POSITIONING
YOUR CHURCH

A Strategy for Developing a Healthy
and Growing Ministry

TERRY L. BATES

Copyright © 2009 by Terry L. Bates
ISBN: 978-0-9816017-9-3
Printed in the United States of America

Published by TQL Press
P.O. Box 892170
Oklahoma City, OK 73189-2170

Graphic Design: Lyn Rayn

DEDICATION

To my wife Robin who has been a faithful companion and co-laborer in our marriage and ministry — no one inspires me more. I cannot imagine attempting what we have endeavored to do for God and His kingdom without her.

To my awesome children Rachael, Naomi and Jason, who have fully supported Robin and me in ministry and fully devoted themselves to Christ in salvation and service. Like the household of Stephanas (I Corinthians 16:15), they have "addicted themselves to the ministry."

To my son-in-law Eric who has joined our family through his marriage to Rachael, whose servant spirit I admire greatly.

To my mom and dad for their life-long investment in my life and ministry, they were my single financial supporters in the beginning of my ministry – Thank You. My mom passed away before this book was published, but her presence and impressions in my life are marked through its pages. My memories of her passionate intercessory prayer life overtake me regularly. To my dad who showed me the value of dedication and a strong work ethic, as well as the significance of early morning devotions as I observed him reading His Bible and praying every morning before going to work. I keep the special memories of the brief time when he also served as my pastor for a season.

To my brother Don, who reminds me so much of my dad for his determination and dedication to work hard, regardless of how tired or even ill he became while battling polycystic kidney disease, just like my mom.

To five awesome congregations that I have had the privilege of being a part of, my home church in Newcastle, Oklahoma; to the church father pastured for a season in Dibble, Oklahoma; to the Harvey Millbrook Church of God (Christian Fellowship Center) in "Hell's Forty Acres" — Fresno, California; to the Cornerstone Church of Fresno, California; and to Faith Church (Faith Tabernacle) in Oklahoma City, Oklahoma. From each of these congregations I have gained significant insights from the opportunities they gave to me to both develop as a leader and to lead in ministry.

To my many great friends who have believed in me, encouraged me and supported me along with way, whom if I started to name, the list would be longer than this book.

To my friend and fellow minister Stan Toler, who encouraged me to write this book and begin a new journey in my life and ministry.

TABLE OF CONTENTS

FOREWORD

Terry Bates is a grower. A friend and ministry colleague, Terry has enriched my life with his godly character and practical insight into turning struggling congregations into vibrant communities of faith. This is a book filled with proven methods for positioning churches for expanded ministries to impact their communities, their nation, and their world.

Terry's ministry has penetrated the four walls of the church to an even wider audience through the media. God has blessed him with an awesome radio, TV, and Internet ministry. And his teaching seminars have made him a pastor to pastors and their staff internationally, teaching them how to use positioning concepts to build stronger congregations and effective leadership.

Of course, growing ministries demand growing budgets. Terry knows how to help with that as well. He has taught thousands of Christian leaders how to raise dollars for building projects, debt retirement, and ministry expansion. He has the ability to identify fundraising trouble spots and provide systems for turning them into viable opportunities for financial growth.

Most of all, Terry Bates is a man of the Word. His powerful preaching and teaching have resulted in changed lives as well as changed organizations. Oklahoma City is a better place because of Terry's defense of the faith. Methods are most effective when they are born from the heart of inspired ministry. From the church platform to the auditorium stage, Terry Bates is constantly helping people grow in spiritual grace and personal vision.

You need this book. You need it because of the times in which we live, and you need it because of the times that are yet to come. The kingdom of God faces challenges that only equipped servants can meet. Terry Bates will give you the tools for being fully equipped in these down-to-earth pages of truth. And his heartwarming stories will give you a glimpse into the kind of person that he is — a man with a heart and mind filled with God's love for others.

—Stan Toler

CHAPTER ONE

JUST CONNECT
THE DOTS!

As a child, I was fascinated by "connect the dots" activities. But instead of simply drawing lines between the numbered dots, I would usually stare at the page first, trying to visualize what the picture might look like when completed. Many times my parents or teachers would say to me, "Just connect the dots!" Eventually I would follow their instructions and see the image come into view that had previously been represented only by a collection of numbered dots.

As my appreciation for "connecting the dots" grew, I discovered some books with connect-the-dots activity pages that had no numbers to follow. With the sequence uncertain, the shape was difficult if not impossible to discern based on the dots alone. There was often a title or a brief description on the page that helped create some potential images in my mind. If not, a quick glance at the answer key always helped!

Ministry in my life has often been like connecting the dots. In many cases, the future of the church I served looked like a bunch of dots on a page that needed connecting. Sometimes, I could find a few numbers to help me navigate the sequence or at least the first few steps that I should take. In other instances, I could see the dots, but there were no numbers and no answer key I could check to see what the image was supposed to look like.

Now, as a ministry consultant, coach, and navigator, my experience with connecting the "dots" often helps come alongside churches and pastors to see the vague image of their vision through the collection of ministry dots. I am privileged to assist them in identifying the sequence that will connect the dots in their ministry and bring forth a clear picture (vision) of their future.

I love the challenge and the opportunity associated with each of these experiences. In many ways, working with these pastors provides the same joy I have experienced when watching my own children work through their connect-the-dots workbooks. It is a priceless thrill to watch people's facial expressions when they finally connect the dots and see the image that had previously been hidden to them.

The GPS (Global Positioning System) that is so widely used today is in many ways an electronic way to connect the dots geographically. It has been used for many years by the government, military, and commercial airlines for aerospace navigation, as well as strategic warfare and defense systems. However, since it was first placed into the hands of everyday people, it has established itself as a vital tool for anyone traveling or delivering goods and services. Those who have received one as a gift from their spouse, or who have used one when renting a car, will say that the GPS has taken some of the challenge out of driving, especially for those who enjoy the thrill of a good adventurous hunt or exploration.

In our childhood education, we read about adventuresome connect-the-dots travelers and explorers in the past who incorporated different measures to create a navigational path for themselves and others to follow. Such measures have included simply breaking a tree branch, stacking stones, or even using pieces of cloth to mark a trail. These processes sometimes became more elaborate as people established landmarks, invested years in creating detailed maps, or learned to navigate their journey using the constellations of the stars and moon at night or by the sun during the day.

The task of navigation has been greatly simplified by the technological advancements of those who created the GPS. It has rapidly become as commonplace as the cell phone, MP3 player, and laptop. Its popularity undoubtedly rose because of curiosity and intrigue, but people have continued to use it because of its practical function.

For all practical purposes, it is simply an interactive electronic map that is designed to guide people from their present position or location to a desired position or location by connecting the dots. Instead of using the paper maps that are so hard to re-fold correctly or maps and directions printed from the internet, today many people speak to or program an electronic device that displays a moving graphic and audibly directs them to their desired destination.

One of the appealing elements of the GPS is that it is customizable. You can start from almost any recognizable address and be guided to almost any other recognizable address. I stress *almost any* simply because I have had the privilege of arguing with a GPS on several occasions. It failed to lead me to my desired location and insisted that it was right and I was wrong, often repeating the word, "Recalculating." In addition, I've travelled with many

One of the appealing elements of the GPS is that it is customizable.

of my friends down long roads that lead to nowhere. That's when I turn the device off and go to the nearest gas station, hoping that I can find an attendant who is not directionally challenged or geographically clueless.

To fully appreciate the system, a person must understand that the efficiency of the GPS directional process requires clear communication to one of the twenty-seven earth-orbiting, solar-powered satellites that make two complete rotations around the earth's 12,000-mile circumference every day. At the risk of oversimplifying the process, the satellite receives the request from your device for navigational assistance to the desired location. The satellite pinpoints the location and creates a path from your present position to the desired position using assigned values that have been given to various roads, landmarks, or locations. The end result is typically both visual and audible instructions that will guide you to your destination by "connecting the dots" of your path.

Wouldn't it be great if there were a "Church GPS" system? Think about it. What if there was a device that would allow us to describe the current position of our church (spiritually, financially, organizationally), identify our desired position, and then press a button and begin receiving visual and audible instructions using some previously assigned Church values that have been given to certain decisions or actions. The closest thing we have to a Church GPS system may be a computer that allows us to do endless searches for information that addresses our particular situation and provides some potential strategies to pursue. However, in the most practical sense, this role is fulfilled by a church consultant or navigator who comes alongside a ministry and pastor to help them find their way to their desired level of effectiveness in ministry by helping them connect the dots of ministry.

While there are obvious limitations to electronic systems, they are designed to take the information that exists within a particular source and to mass distribute that information through technology. Before technology, and along with technology, we have also benefited from an abundance of books, as well as audio, and other electronic resources. In addition to technology and printed resources, individuals can receive instruction through human communication and interaction both on a personal level and in a group setting. This human instruction and interaction typically occurs through various educational institutions, conferences, and seminars, or with personal consultants, coaches, or navigators, as individuals of experience and expertise share their valuable insights.

I must not fail to acknowledge that the greatest guidance system in my life has been the Holy Spirit.

I have benefited from all of the above resources at various times in my life. In fact, I decided to share my experiences and insights in this book, in various public settings, and as a church consultant or navigator, based on my hope and desire that individuals and ministries could benefit in some way from my God-given gift and desire to connect the dots in ministry. However, I must not fail to acknowledge that the greatest guidance system in my life has been the Holy Spirit. I don't want to sound hyperspiritual, nor do I want to ignore the fact that the Holy Spirit has been my greatest teacher, guide, and navigator. Throughout my ministry, whenever I have prayed and asked for wisdom and understanding, I have found it. Sometimes this insight has come in the form of a keen understanding that was given to me through direct inspiration or by studying scripture or the writings of other great leaders. Other times the insight has come through a relationship with a consultant or navigator where the Holy Spirit illuminated my understanding and I was able to connect the dots in my specific situation.

I have asked the Holy Spirit to guide me in sharing the experiences and insights from my own life and ministry, as well as from all of the pastors, leaders, and churches that I have had the privilege of partnering with as a consultant, coach, and navigator. But I have also asked the Holy Spirit to guide me in sharing the timeless and eternal principles that are recorded in the Bible and to help you personalize them for your particular situation.

As a pastor, teacher and leader, you have undoubtedly had the experience in which you shared a message or taught a lesson to a group of people only to have people approach you afterwards to explain how the message or lesson you shared was "just for them." Many times when this happens, I am amazed at how the application of what I shared was interpreted and applied to different people with very different experiences or situations. My prayer in writing this book and every time I speak is that the Holy Spirit will personalize and customize the principles and experiences that are shared, so that each person can clearly see the application to their specific situation and that it will produce a clear strategy for implementation as they discover how to connect the dots in their ministry.

CHAPTER TWO

UNDERSTANDING AND DEFINING CHURCH HEALTH

It is important that we provide a foundation for our perspective and understanding of church health and church growth. To do so, we will explore a brief overview of the statistical definitions of church health and church growth, as well as a spiritual and biblical perspective of church health.

STATISTICAL DEFINITIONS OF CHURCH HEALTH

Through my involvement with hundreds of churches, after completing my assessment as a consultant, I typically classify a church in one of six ways.

DECLINING CHURCHES

Declining churches are the first category of churches that need positioning (or repositioning) in order to develop an effective and sustainable turnaround strategy.

In my work with these churches, I have applied the statistical definition of a *declining church* as any church that has declined in attendance or

income by at least three percent or more each year for three or more consecutive years. For example, a church that has declined in attendance
from one hundred to ninety-six, then to ninety-two, and finally to eighty-
nine over a three-year period of time is statistically defined as a *declining
church*. Or if a church's income has declined from $100,000 to $96,000
to $92,000 to $89,000 over a three-year period, it is statistically defined
as a declining church.

**Our estimates indicate that between fifty and sixty percent of the
300,000 evangelical churches in America are in statistical decline,** with
the causes associated with their decline almost as varied as the number of
different churches. There are many contributing factors of decline, such as
demographic shift, church division, transfer of members, relocation of the
church or employers, congregational deaths, and more. However, regardless
of what the contributing factors may be, the one absolute cause for decline
is an inability to reach and retain
more new people than the number of
people exiting the ministry.

> Every church is going to have
> some level of natural attrition.

Every church is going to have
some level of natural attrition. This
attrition rate will vary depending on the developments in a community,
but the typical attrition rate is around five percent per year. Therefore, in
order for a church to grow consistently, it must reach and retain an average of eight new people for every five people that it loses—and it must
do it every year.

PLATEAUED CHURCHES

Plateaued churches are the second group that need positioning (or
repositioning) in order to develop an effective, sustainable, *fresh start*
strategy.

For the purposes of our assessments, I have statistically defined a
plateaued church as any church that has neither declined nor increased in
attendance or income by more than three percent each year for three or
more consecutive years. For example, a church in this group that started
with an attendance of one hundred or even 1,000 during the three-year

period has not declined below ninety or 900, nor has it grown beyond 110 or 1,100 respectively over a three-year period. Or, if a church's annual income was $100,000 or $1,000,000; their annual income did not decline below $90,000 or $900,000; or rise above $110,000 or $1,100,000 respectively over a three-year period.

Our estimates indicate that approximately thirty percent of the 300,000 evangelical churches in America are in a statistical plateau. There are a number of contributing factors that may enable this ministry to barely stay above the margin of decline, but often these same contributing factors are preventing the ministry from progressing into a healthier growth environment.

To the credit of these ministries, they have demonstrated the ability to either replace the losses that have occurred within their ministry within a reasonable time or their community and congregation are equally stagnant with no present signs of deterioration or growth.

It should also be pointed out that in most cases (with some smaller rural churches being the exception), churches do not remain on a plateau for more than five years before either entering a season of decline, until they reach a new lower plateau, or a season of growth or until they reach a higher plateau. In a smaller percentage of these churches, a recent change in pastoral leadership, growth in the community, or some other intentional steps of outreach have been implemented, resulting in either a new growth pattern in the church, or possibly a higher level of plateau.

LAZARUS CHURCH

A third type of church can be identified as a *Lazarus church*. In my personal research, I have statistically defined this group as a church that has been on the verge of closing or it has been closed for some period of time (typically because of a pattern of decline). After this period of time, the church has been restarted or reopened by a new pastor and usually includes some portion of the previous members. Although they may be experiencing an initial surge of growth and new life, because the previous members spent several years in the church when it was declining and dying, they don't know quite how to function or act with this new life and health. These *Lazarus churches* need positioning in order to develop an effective, sustainable, *Restart* strategy. Our research indicates that only about **one percent of the churches in America meet the criteria of a *Lazarus church*.**

It should be pointed out that even Jesus did not resurrect everyone at the cemeteries that he visited. He was selective and specifically called them by name. This possibly illustrates that not every church that is dying or has been closed should in fact be brought back to life. In some cases, these ministries may in fact need to die and either allow the assets and resources to be used to fund a completely new ministry group to start a new life cycle for the church or relocate the ministry to a new area that best matches the gifts and passion of the pastor and congregation. In some cases, a previous population center may have evaporated, requiring the relocation of the ministry to a growing community, simply on the basis of good stewardship of resources.

When I think about these Lazarus churches, I compare them to someone who may have been diagnosed with a terminal disease and gradually declines in health to the point that hospice care is approved for them. In many cases, the assignment of a hospice worker is to simply make a dying person's last days as comfortable as possible in an environment that they prefer.

> It should be pointed out that even Jesus did not resurrect everyone at the cemeteries that he visited.

I have observed many cases in which the hospice worker was assigned and the patient was expected to pass away within a few months. I've actually seen terminal individuals quit their jobs under doctor's encouragement in order to see all of the people and places they could afford to see during their final days. However, somewhere along the way, they experienced the miracle of divine healing. As a result, they no longer qualified for hospice care or any form of disability compensation. This meant they had to go job hunting again, because they had given up their job instead of taking a medical leave.

I've watched individuals such as this have to rebuild their lives after thinking their life was over. It's not easy to go back into the job market, possibly repurchase a home, or rent a place to live, many times at an older age. After embracing a view of impending death and learning how to die with dignity, these healed individuals need to adjust to their new life and learn how to live again.

In the same way, Lazarus churches need help positioning (or repositioning) for their new life. Without this help, the new life in the church will not be sustainable for an extended period of time, and the church will once again become a plateaued church or declining church.

BARRIER CHURCH

A fourth type of church can be identified as a *barrier church*. Barrier churches are vibrant and growing churches that need help breaking a growth or size barrier (100, 200, 500, 750, 1000, and so on). Their inability to break through a barrier and sustain growth indicates they are facing an invisible barrier.

In my personal assessments, I have statistically defined a *barrier church* as a ministry that experiences upward seasonal and cyclical swings in attendance between three and ten percent on a regular basis, but they cannot sustain the growth for an extended period of time.

In the beginning of the calendar year, the church may average one hundred or even 1,000 in attendance. Through the engagement of an intentional spring outreach emphasis, the church may increase by three percent or more for the second and third quarters. In the fall, another outreach emphasis may add yet another three percent or more increase. However, within a few short months, the church returns to the original reference point of either one hundred or 1,000 respectively.

One of the primary differences between *barrier churches* and *plateaued churches* is that barrier churches seldom drop below their base attendance and often experience seasonal growth points in excess of three percent or more, possibly on multiple occasions, before returning back to the lower base attendance. Within a short period of time, they will move into yet another season of growth. However, since they have not implemented a strategy to sustain the new growth, they simply return to their base attendance again.

It is obvious that these churches seem to be hitting an invisible ceiling in their growth, which prevents them from going to the next level of ministry size, even though they have sufficiently vibrant and healthy ministries with which to produce these seasons of growth.

These barrier churches need positioning in order to develop a *breakthrough strategy* that will enable them to enter into a larger ministry size—not only to sustain the new level, but also to continue to grow through future size barriers.

We estimate that between five and ten percent of all evangelical churches in America are barrier churches and with sufficient coaching and consultation, are the most likely group of churches to become *growing churches* **that break through multiple barriers.**

GROWING CHURCHES

A fifth type of church can be identified as a *growing church*. For the purposes of my assessments, I have defined a *growing church* as a ministry that has a three percent or more increase in attendance *and* giving each year for at least three years. These churches need a positioning strategy that will enable them to continually expand their ministry infrastructure so it will accommodate the continual growth. Best estimates indicate that only ten percent of all evangelical churches in America meet these specific parameters.

Within this classification of *growing churches* there are two primary types. **First, there are churches that are growing primarily through the transfer of members or believers from other churches.** Many times the growth of these churches is at the expense of declining churches, whose members are transferring into the growing churches that are providing more ministry opportunities and resources for families. Every indication is that one half of all growing churches (or five percent of all evangelical churches) are growing primarily as a result of transfer growth.

The second group of *growing churches* **includes those whose primary growth is the result of conversion growth and evangelistic efforts.** The fact remains that it is possible to have a growing church using church growth techniques that simply attract people—many of whom are believers from other churches. However, there is another fact established. Approximately one half of all *growing churches* are in fact reaching unbelievers, the un-churched and the de-churched, and they are bringing these individuals into a personal relationship with Jesus Christ. My personal passion is to help every church become a *growing church*, primarily through conversion growth, not transfer growth.

However, we must not ignore the fact that churches that are growing by conversion growth will also attract believers, primarily because these believers want to be a part of an evangelistic church. Evangelistic excitement and passion attracts both the believer and unbeliever. This is especially true of the young families that are making their way into churches across America. They are looking for a church that has an evangelistic passion, relevant music, and ministry of the Word, along with quality ministries and ministry environments for their children and family.

Both types of growing churches will face a specific set of challenges that will require positioning or repositioning. For example, churches that are growing primarily from transfers will face the challenge of having people become a part of their church who have established expectations as to how the church and pastor should function. They will compare the various aspects of their selective church experiences to their current place of involvement and find a way to introduce their preferences or ideas. However, churches that are growing primarily as the result of conversions will face the challenge of having new people who do not have any established understanding as to how the church, pastor, or believers should function. Both situations create their own specific set of challenges that can be successfully addressed through a strategic Ministry Action Plan (MAP).

> Approximately one half of all *growing churches* are in fact reaching unbelievers, the un-churched and the de-churched.

NEW CHURCHES

The sixth type of church or church group consists of *new churches*. My personal experience as a church planter, the pastor of a church that sponsored many other new churches, and a consultant has caused me to define a *new church* as one that is less than five years old and that is growing by at least twenty percent each year. The standard of at least twenty percent each year should be much easier to meet in new churches for a number of valid reasons.

First, new churches naturally create new excitement and new entry points for both new and existing believers. Once a new church secures a solid core group of believers, it should be able to increase by at least twenty percent each year. If not, what exists may not truly be a new church; it may simply be a *disenfranchised group* from another church; a *well-intentioned, but not adequately gifted group* sent out from another church or launched independently of a sponsoring church, or possibly even a church that has *relocated* with the hope of being identified as a *new church*, while embracing all of the previous systems and structures of ministry.

When an existing church relocates, it cannot be considered a *new church* unless it has purged itself of any previous baggage and historical identity and truly embraced a new form of ministry and leadership. If this is not done, when new people arrive expecting to be a part of something new and fresh, they will still smell the mothballs of old ministry lingering in the atmosphere. If a church group has relocated with the intent of being a new church, but it is not experiencing at least twenty percent growth each year, this is an indication that they only have a new location and possibly a new name, but they are the same church. In such cases, the church would best be described by one of the previous definitions.

We also recognize that every church that relocates does not necessarily want to be considered a new church. They may simply want to be an existing church with a new location. In this case, the church may more appropriately be considered a *growing church*, if it is experiencing a growth rate of at least three percent per year. Their current growth may have necessitated a new location, but there is no need or desire to be identified as a new church.

We must also point out that if a new church has begun, but it is not growing by at least twenty percent each year in its first five years (and it is not a pre-existing church that has relocated with a goal of some type of ministry makeover), then there may be serious health questions regarding the viability of the ministry. It is possible that there was a *premature birth or launch* before the group was ready to go public. It is also possible that there was a *stillborn* experience, in which the launch or birth of the church possessed no life-giving capacity. In such cases, there may be a body (church group), but there are no detectable signs of life. Yet another possibility may be the attempt to start a new church without a sponsoring church or agency, therefore lacking the prayer support, spiritual and emotional support, relational and mentoring support, and financial support needed for an effective launch.

There are many other possibilities that might be addressed in regards to a perceived new church that is not growing or possibly even declining within the first five years of its existence, most of which are beyond the scope of this specific work, but will be addressed in future projects.

A second reason that new churches should easily achieve a growth rate of at least twenty percent or more each year can be attributed to the significant amount of time, energy, and resources that can be devoted to evangelism and outreach during the first five years. In the early stages of a new church, there are fewer expectations for a multifaceted ministry or a broad menu of ministry programming. People who participate in new churches have chosen to have fewer options at the beginning in order to allow the ministry to focus on growth. While these new people eventually want the basic ministry options needed for their family, such as early childhood or nursery ministry, children's ministry, music and worship ministries, life groups or fellowship groups, and possibly even youth ministry, they don't expect a new church to offer all of the ministry options that a larger and more established ministry may provide or be expected to provide.

> One of the most significant reasons that new churches grow so fast in the first few years is because almost all of their time, energy, and resources, that later become committed to sustaining ministries, are initially devoted to evangelism and outreach.

In fact, one of the most significant reasons that new churches grow so fast in the first few years is because almost all of their time, energy, and resources, that later become committed to *sustaining ministries*, are initially devoted to evangelism and outreach. The longer a church is in existence (unless there is some intentionality to do otherwise), the more time, energy, and resources will shift to maintenance and care of people, as well as ministries and facilities, resulting in a reduced amount of these elements for evangelism and church growth. Inherently, with only a few exceptions, as the church matures, the focus shifts from evangelism and outreach ministries to discipleship and pastoral care ministries. This shift ultimately causes the church to be reclassified by one of the other five categories.

SPIRITUAL AND BIBLICAL DEFINITIONS OF CHURCH HEALTH

In my personal involvement in church health and church growth for over thirty years, there has been a very foundational perspective that has enabled me to define church health from a spiritual and biblical perspective.

The most common expression by which the spiritual health of God's people can be described is the comparison to a healthy human body.

In the scriptures, we are provided with an almost identical image of church health in both the Old Testament and the New Testament. The most common expression by which the spiritual health of God's people can be described is the comparison to a healthy human body. Undoubtedly, your mind has begun to race through the Bible, recalling many scriptures verses that make this contrast or comparison. I will draw from two primary passages of scripture to illustrate this principle.

First, in Ezekiel 37, the spiritual health of the nation or whole house of Israel is described in Ezekiel's vision of the valley of dry bones. In this vision, God speaks to Ezekiel and instructs him to prophesy to the bones to illustrate God's plan of spiritual restoration. As Ezekiel prophesies to the bones, the process of restored spiritual health begins with bone connecting to bone, followed by the sinews and flesh coming up on the newly formed skeleton, and then being covered by skin. Finally, Ezekiel is told to prophesy to the wind, which represents the Holy Spirit, and commands the wind to breathe upon them so they may live.

From this vision, we can identify four key components of church and ministry health.

SKELETAL STRUCTURE

The foundation of church and ministry health begins with the skeletal infrastructure of ministry. The skeleton in this vision or illustration represents the leadership, organizational, and foundational infrastructure of the church. The size, strength, and expansion or growth of the skeletal infrastructure will significantly impact the health of the church. The growth of the church and the ministry capacity of the church cannot exceed the capacity of the skeletal frame or infrastructure.

In all of my studies on church health and church growth, I do not personally recall anyone addressing the skeletal infrastructure as the core of church health. However, when God places this vision before Ezekiel regarding the spiritual health of the nation of Israel, he begins with the skeletal infrastructure.

The concept is simple and yet extremely significant. Without a strong skeletal infrastructure there cannot be a healthy church body that is mobilized for the purpose of God. If you remove the skeletal framework from our human bodies, there is no framework on which to attach the muscular system, nervous system, circulatory system, vital organs, or even the skin. Without a strong skeletal infrastructure, at best the church could only be illustrated as a blood-pumping blob, with no ability to be mobilized or engaged in the purpose of God. Unfortunately, this does in fact describe many ministries that have many of the other components represented in this illustration (sinews, skin and Spirit), but lack sufficient infrastructure to mobilize their efforts.

In my perspective, the skeletal infrastructure represents the leadership, organizational, and foundational structure of the church that is necessary to tie all of the other components of the ministry

together. Therefore the skeleton would represent such things as leadership, administration, and organizational systems. I also believe the skeleton represents the prayer- and Word-foundation of the church. All of the core or foundational elements needed to sustain the ministry of the church are a part of the skeletal infrastructure.

The skeleton in the human body can be compared to the foundation and footings of a construction project, whether it is a residential home or a major skyscraper. The size of the building that is to be built determines the size of the foundation and footings that must be created. The foundation and footings required for a single story home are not as deep or strong as the foundation and footings required for a skyscraper. In construction, the higher or wider you want to go, the deeper, stronger and wider you have to go with the foundation. When there is a desire to expand an additional structure either horizontally or vertically with another floor or level, the project requires either expanding the foundation horizontally or reinforcing the foundation under the existing floor in order to support the weight of the additional structure.

> The size of the frame determines the size of the person and the "load limits" that they can handle.

We seem to understand the importance of expanding and reinforcing construction foundations before we expand, and yet many ministries never consider what ministry infrastructure must be expanded in order to sustain and support the ministry expansion that is desired. In the illustration of the human body, medical doctors readily acknowledge that the skeletal frame of an eight-year-old child cannot support the weight or load that can be carried by a six foot adult. The size of the frame determines the size of the person and the "load limits" that they can handle. In many cases, the health problems of the skeletal or bone structure that people experience are the direct result of a weight or stress overload on their skeletal frame.

Ministries must understand that ministry infrastructure must be expanded or reinforced in order to sustain and support expansion of ministry. This means that *before* a church adds new ministries or new worship services or new worship locations, it should first expand the prayer base, establish the Biblical foundation for ministry, recruit and train new leadership and ministry partners, and modify and expand the administrative and organizational infrastructure of the church. Churches that invest time in these areas of constantly expanding and reinforcing their ministry infrastructure increase their capacity to expand ministry. Churches that are growing must be proactive in expanding all of these areas, much like the New Testament leaders did when they established the new ministry of deacons to allow for the expansion and growth of church—and it worked (Acts 6).

Ministry infrastructure is not very exciting, and that's why it is often overlooked and ignored. In the same way, foundations and footings in construction are not very exciting; that's why there is not a "Parade of Foundations" or other special tours to inspect and admire the foundations of construction projects. Instead we have the Parade of Homes, grand opening celebrations, and open house events when projects are completed, simply because people get excited about the finished work, not the infrastructure.

The comparison doesn't end there. Consider how much time, energy, and resources are spent enhancing and preparing the physical appearance of our human bodies. Compare that to the amount of time that is spent

> A healthy and growing ministry begins with a healthy and expanding skeletal infrastructure.

strengthening our skeletal frame, until or unless there is a fracture, break, or other bone weakness that must be addressed. Ministries are notorious for spending tremendous amounts of time, energy, and resources to make sure the visible presentations of ministry are well presented, but make a very small investment in the ongoing health and expansion of their ministry infrastructure. A healthy and growing ministry begins with a healthy and expanding skeletal infrastructure.

SINEWS OR MINISTRY SYSTEMS

The sinews represent the various internal organs and operating systems within the human body, which are attached to the skeletal frame. These can be compared to the various ministries of the church, both the visible ministries as well as the hidden ministries of the church.

Just as the human body is dependent upon the various internal organs and operating systems, such as the circulatory system, nervous or sensory system, and muscular system, **the church is dependent upon the various ministries of the church to provide life-giving sources, as well as mobility and function.** When a human body has a diseased or unhealthy internal organ, the entire body suffers until the organ's health is restored; or if necessary, artificial health is provided until an organ transplant can be provided. In the same way, when there is a problem within the ministries of the church (internal organs or ministries), the entire church body suffers until the health is restored; or in some cases a "ministry transplant" is needed. A ministry transplant might be the need to replace an ineffective ministry or ministry format with a different ministry or ministry format.

We all understand the significance of the circulatory system within the body. Through proper circulation of the blood, oxygen is carried through the body with life-giving capacity. **It is my view that ministries that provide fellowship and relationship building opportunities accomplish this purpose in the church.** When there is a lack of quality fellowship and relationship building that energizes and refreshes people emotionally and socially, ministry fatigue will result. In addition, when there are conflicts and strife within the church, these serve as "circulatory blockages" that interfere with the healthy flow of loving relationships and produce spiritual cardiac arrests within the ministry.

When the "sensing ability" of the church is unhealthy, it prevents the church body from seeing, hearing, touching, and caring.

When the nervous system or sensory system of the body is unhealthy, the church becomes insensitive to the needs of others, unaware of ministry guests who are searching for a place of caring ministry, and unable to provide adequate care and support for those within the body of Christ. Do you recall the reflex tests often administered by the doctor, or perhaps you have either experienced or observed a doctor testing a patient's levels of sensitivity to touch? We can easily acknowledge the impact of weak vision or even reduced hearing capacity. When the "sensing ability" of the church is unhealthy, it prevents the church body from seeing, hearing, touching, and caring for the needs of those who are within their sphere of influence, causing the body to be unhealthy in ministry.

> I believe it is important to have an effective or healthy ministry that enables a church to impact the lives of those who identify with their style and preferences.

Although the illustration could be pressed in many ways, we must acknowledge the significance of the muscular system, which provides movement and mobility to the overall ministry. **Developing the ministry muscles of the church involves developing the ministry gifts and skills of those within the church.** If the church does not go beyond *identifying* believers' spiritual gifts and abilities and invest in *developing* these gifts and skills, the ministry muscles of the church become weakened and ineffective.

Ultimately, the healthy mobility and function of the church is represented by these "sinews," which must be healthy and developed in order for the church to function properly and effectively.

SKIN OR STYLES/PERSONALITY

The skin or flesh represents the personality, identity, styles, preferences, and various demographics of ministry. Human skin not only reflects broad diversity of races and languages, it also becomes a part of our individual identity. The skin that came upon the bones and sinews in Ezekiel's vision revealed Israel's identity.

When I apply this representation to church health, I believe it represents ministry that is culturally relevant and demographically compatible to the people within the scope of the ministry's sphere of influence. If a church ignores the culture, demographics, styles, and preferences of the people they are trying to reach, the ministry could be considered unhealthy or ineffective. However, when a ministry becomes comfortable in their "skin" and is effective in reaching people through their unique personality, styles, preferences, and demographics, then the church would be considered healthy.

At the risk of being misunderstood, I believe it is important to have an effective or healthy ministry that enables a church to impact the lives of those who identify with their style and preferences. I also believe it is important to have ministries with various "ages" of skin (children, youth, young adults, mid-life adults, older adults). Where demographically justified and the church has the ability to do so, a healthy church will also provide ministries that reach to diverse language groups and other preferences, interests, or needs that may exist within their community.

SPIRIT OR THE GOD FACTOR

The prophet Ezekiel makes an obvious and yet profound observation. After prophesying to the bones, sinews, and flesh, the bodies were completely constructed, but there was no life or breath in them. While there is a necessity to have a sufficient skeletal infrastructure, ministry and muscle sinews that provide mobility and function, and ministry skin to provide personality, distinction, and cultural relevance, it is possible to have all of the systems, structures, and styles and still have not life, breath, or Spirit.

> God has an order and a design to everything.

Make no mistake about it. I passionately believe that every healthy church needs the skeleton, sinews, and skin; **but if the Spirit of God does not breathe upon what we have, it is still dead and lifeless.** At the same time, there are ministries that place all of their emphasis on the "Spirit factor" and completely ignore the fact that, when God communicated His plan to raise up the nation of Israel as a mighty influence in the land, He did not begin with the Spirit, He began with the skeleton.

God has an order and a design to everything. He revealed to Ezekiel that it always begins with the skeleton, sinews, and skin before He breathes the Spirit upon them. This was the same pattern that God demonstrated in forming man out of the dust of earth—first shaping the man (skeleton, sinews, and skin), before breathing into his nostrils with the breath of God.

Likewise, when God wanted to give Adam a companion, He put Adam to sleep and He began construction with a rib—a part of the skeletal system.

It is without question in my mind that if more churches and ministries could understand the process of beginning with the skeletal ministry infrastructure, then adding the sinews of ministry systems, and finally the skin's distinctive and unique identity and personality, then God could effectively breath His Spirit upon their preparation, and it would produce the same result as revealed in Ezekiel's vision: "So I prophesied as he commanded me, and the breath came into them, and they lived and stood up upon their feet, an exceeding great army." (Ezekiel 37:10)

THE APOSTLE PAUL'S VIEW OF A HEALTHY CHURCH

In Paul's writings to the church at Corinth, he also draws from the illustration of the human body to communicate what a healthy church body looks like and how it functions. In 1 Corinthians 12, Paul details the overall health, interworking, interdependence, function, and mobilization of the body of Christ, as he reminds us that there are many members, but one body. Each member (believer or ministry) needs the other members (believers or ministries) in order to be complete and healthy. The parallel between Paul's illustration and Ezekiel's vision is easily seen.

Paul also uses another valuable reference to the human body to describe the role of those with leadership gifts in equipping believers for the work of ministry. To the church at Ephesus, Paul writes

11. And he gave some, apostles; and some, prophets; and some, evangelists; and some, pastors and teachers;
12. For the perfecting of the saints, for the work of the ministry, for the edifying of the body of Christ:
13. Till we all come in the unity of the faith, and of the knowledge of the Son of God, unto a perfect man, unto the measure of the stature of the fulness of Christ:

Ephesians 4:11–13 (KJV)

The Apostle Paul not only brings in the reference "unto a perfect (complete, healthy, whole) man," but he also reveals one of the key functions of those in leadership capacities. The phrase "perfecting of the saints" is associated with a word picture in the Greek language. The word *perfecting* is often translated as *equipping* which is included in its interpretation. However, the word picture created by Paul's selection of words is literally the image of someone who is suffering from a dislocated joint or bone.

It is easy to see the impact of pain and immobilization that occurs to the rest of a person's body when they are experiencing the excruciating pain of a dislocated shoulder or other bone or joint. In the same way, when believers are "dislocated" or not in their proper place—properly connected to a healthy body—then the whole body suffers. Not only does the entire body feel the pain and suffering associated with a specific area of the body being affected, but it also severely impairs the mobilization of the rest of the body. The same is true in the body of Christ.

> Those in ministry leadership (apostle, prophet, evangelist, pastor, and teacher) are to repair the area that is dislocated.

Paul's descriptive words create a healthy solution to an otherwise unhealthy body. Those in ministry leadership (apostle, prophet, evangelist, pastor, and teacher) are to repair the area that is dislocated. The word picture for *perfecting* in this text literally means "straightening out the disjointed." Just as a medical doctor would reset the dislocation in the human body, allowing the body to restore health and mobilization, the role of leaders in the church is to "straighten out the disjointed."

When believers in a church are not plugged in to ministry and connected to others in relationships and ministry partnership, they are "disjointed." This causes the entire body or ministry to suffer and the mobilization of the rest of the body or ministry is affected by the parts of the body (members or ministries) that are dislocated or disjointed from the rest of the body.

This further explains Paul's next declaration:

15. But speaking the truth in love, may *grow up* into him in all things, which is the head, even Christ:

16. From whom *the whole body fitly joined together* and *compacted by that which every joint supplieth*, according *to the effectual working in the measure of every part, maketh increase of the body* unto the edifying of itself in love.

Ephesians 4:15-16 (KJV)

Paul clearly sees the health of the church being illustrated in the health of a human body, which grows, is joined together, supplies what is needed, effectively works together, and makes increase of the body.

Both Ezekiel and Paul describe *positioning* in their illustrations. As bones join to bones, sinews and skin and Spirit come together; and as leaders work to "straighten out the disjointed," so the work of the ministry can be accomplished, the body of Christ can grow (mature), be mobilized, minister together, and increase the body (size, numerically). This is positioning and *connecting the dots* of the church for ministry health and growth.

CHAPTER THREE

WHAT DOES "POSITIONING" HAVE TO DO WITH A CHURCH?

Positioning is still a relatively new term to the world of ministry, yet its relevance is undeniable and its application is critical to the effectiveness and impact of the local church. While new to the world of ministry, the concept of positioning is not new to society. In fact, positioning has been the key to many businesses succeeding and the absence of positioning has been the reason for many others failing.

The danger of reading too quickly through this next segment or lightly skimming over it is that you may have a limited or an impaired understanding of positioning as it relates to the business world and then try to apply your level of understanding to your church or ministry and feel that is sufficient. In reality, many churches and ministries have in fact taken only one aspect of positioning and applied it their organizations and efforts, only to be puzzled as to why it didn't work for them.

> Positioning has been the key to many businesses succeeding.

Most individuals have the limited perspective that *positioning* is just another word for *branding* or *marketing*. Admittedly, one aspect of positioning does in fact deal with branding and marketing. For most businesses this would be better understood as *external or social positioning*. However, *full positioning* encompasses both external positioning and internal positioning. When you fail to engage in full positioning or full repositioning internally and externally, the results of only engaging in one or the other will produce disappointing and frustrating results.

In our earlier reference to the GPS, the value of full positioning can be understood by understanding that the electronic device must identify its current position (where you are) and the desired position (where you want to be). But full positioning doesn't end there. As an individual begins to follow the instructions provided by the GPS, there is constant *repositioning* (or as the recorded voice might often say, "recalculating") along the way. In the same way, knowing where you are today and identifying where you want to be is not enough. Things in ministry constantly change. Therefore, **as you begin moving from the starting point to the destination, you must begin the journey of movement, constantly repositioning and recalculating along the way.** The principles that you will find in this book are designed to help you through the continual repositioning and recalculating process.

EXTERNAL POSITIONING FOR CHURCHES

Since every church and ministry exists within a society of people, it must make its presence known to the people of their society through external positioning. Many terms have been associated with this process, but the most common are *marketing* and *branding*. While some people are uncomfortable with the concept of church or ministry marketing, branding, or even positioning, the reality is that every church and ministry does external positioning in some way and to some degree. The only question is whether or not they are effective in their efforts.

External positioning may take on a variety of forms and degrees of complexity. The *first* and most simplistic forms include verbal recommendations, personal endorsements, and testimonials based on personal experience. Secondary forms of awareness are based on what they have heard from individuals they are personally acquainted with or from market awareness, which is based on their perceptions that have been formed by the intentional and unintentional external positioning efforts of the church.

Higher **degrees of complexity are primarily based on a greater level of investment of time and resources, coupled with the incorporation of various forms of media.** Beyond a personal or verbal recommendation, a second degree of positioning would include some form of print materials, such as direct mail, personal invite cards, business cards, print advertisement in publications, external signage, external banners, and billboards.

A *third* **degree of complexity would incorporate electronic technology, such as websites, digital message boards, Internet audio or video messages, radio or television ads or programming, e-mail, e-newsletters, and text-messaging.** Today's technology would also include webcasting, streaming video, or archived online videos.

A *fourth* **degree of complexity would involve events conducted and services provided for the benefit of the community, which introduce the church or ministry to the participants.** These events and services are designed to engage the community to interact with the people and programming provided by the church or ministry. These may include compassion services, such as a food pantry, benevolence clothing room, Mother's Day Out program, specialized support programs to assist single parents or families, emotional support programs, addiction-free support groups, community health or exercise classes, recreational sports ministries, seasonal celebration events (Easter, Christmas, etc.), annual projects (back-to-school supplies, coats for kids, canned food drive for a local food bank), weddings, funerals, graduation ceremonies, and more.

A *fifth* **degree of external positioning might incorporate a** *third place ministry***, which is a somewhat neutral or alternative space that is dedicated to bridging the church to the community and the community to the church.** Some of these spaces may have a Starbucks feel to them, while others may exist as recreational centers, exercise or health centers, support-group centers, activity centers, and any other form of socially, non-threatening environment. The idea of the *third place* is to create a non-threatening, need-meeting, social networking environment where relationships can be developed and ministry can be provided. The term *third place* originates from the concept that the first two places in a person's life are their home and workplace. Most people turn to a third place for their social interaction. If churches and ministries can create *third place ministries*, they can develop relationships with these individuals. In fact, when you examine the ministry of Jesus, you will discover that Jesus conducted most of His ministry in a *third place* environment.

A *sixth* degree of external positioning is also accomplished through multi-site campuses or satellite churches. These multiple venues serve as way for a church to directly impact and engage a specific segment group of people. These multi-site campuses are similar to the cell-based ministry or even the house-church ministry in that they bring the ministry to a more defined or specific demographic or community of people. However, they are very different in that they are much larger than a cell group or house church, often offering many of the ministries of the main campus within their specific geographic or social environment.

> Through external positioning activities, a church or ministry not only increases awareness of its existence, but it also becomes branded or associated with certain activities and events.

Undoubtedly, many other forms of external positioning could be identified. While churches and ministries may resist the idea of referring to these activities as marketing or branding, the reality suggests differently. As a result of the activities of the church there comes an increased awareness of the church, whether it is intentional or unintentional. *Increased awareness* is one of the primary goals of any marketing or branding strategy.

Through external positioning activities, a church or ministry not only increases awareness of its existence, but it also becomes branded or associated with certain activities and events. They may become known as "the church with a community sports program," "the church with a Mother's Day Out program," "the church with a food and clothing ministry," "the church with a support group ministry for people with former additions," or any number of distinctives which are also known as *branding*.

It is important to understand that external positioning should create a *ministry bridge* or *bridge ministry* to encourage the people of the church or ministry to go out from the meeting place in order to engage and embrace the culture and connect to the community around them. As they engage and embrace the culture and community, new relationships will be formed that will allow them to invite individuals to walk with them across the ministry bridge to experience the community of faith that awaits them. In addition, establishing bridge ministries that are open to the community will create multiple entry points for people to have exposure to the people and passion of church, without making a commitment to the community of faith itself.

Although some people consider this unhealthy, the reality is that this is exactly what Jesus recommended in Matthew 5:16: "In the same way, let your light shine before men, that they may see your good deeds and praise your Father in heaven." It must be understood that we should not be engaged in external positioning for the purpose of bringing some special glory or honor to ourselves, but rather to use these activities and services to point people to Jesus as our motivation for caring, concern, and compassion.

We must recognize that simply engaging in external positioning and failing to address the need for *internal positioning* will ultimately lead in a failure to adequately meet the needs of people. This reality can be illustrated in a story about a company that wanted to introduce a new dog food product, with an ultimate goal of securing the greatest share of the dog food market.

To accomplish their goal they needed to implement an effective external positioning strategy. To do so, they engaged the services of a research agency to observe the dog food buying decisions and patterns of dog owners and to assist them in designing a label or identity that would appeal to dog owners. After months of interviewing dog food buyers in retail outlets, they presented their findings to a graphics department to design the label or identity for their product.

When the graphics department completed their work it was presented to the corporate leaders, who applauded their work and approved the design. The product was labeled and quickly shipped to retailers. The first three months that the product was available it set amazing sales records and captured the largest share of the market in an unprecedented time frame. However, over the next few months, product sales fell rapidly and became almost non-existent.

When the second quarter reports were released, the corporate leaders immediately contacted the research agency and asked them to conduct another survey to discover why people were not purchasing the product. The research team was dispatched to their various locations and within a very brief time they were able to ascertain the problem. They recorded their findings and prepared to present their report to the corporate leaders.

When the research representatives appeared in the corporate board-room to present their findings, the corporate leaders immediately began questioning them about their previous recommendations that influenced the graphic designs and marketing label. The research team vigorously defended their findings, presenting irrefutable evidence from the surveys that people loved the labels and found them both compelling and hard to resist when they were making their purchasing decisions.

Upon review of this evidence, the corporate leaders then insisted on knowing why their product rose so quickly, only to have fallen in popularity equally as fast. The research team was now ready to present their findings, to which they reported: "The answer to the question regarding the rapid decline in the purchase of your product is simple: dogs won't eat it!"

This illustrates the reality that many businesses, as well as many churches and ministries spend an extraordinary amount of time and energy in the area of external positioning only to discover that when people do arrive, they simply don't like what they find. All of their efforts and invest-ment on creating awareness, identity, and invitation were in vain because they had not given adequate consideration to what was on the inside.

I admit we must be careful with this illustration. In the case of dog food, a secondary research project should have been undertaken that would have exposed a variety of dogs to their product until they created a quality product that dogs would eat. However, this is not necessarily true of the church. We should not necessarily conduct a research project to find out what people like and shape ministry exclusively on this basis. This is "consumerism" in its purest form.

To exclusively implement a consumerist approach might be acceptable in some secular business strategies, but churches and ministries must remain true to their true mission and "reason-for-being" as declared by God. While this is true, there is nothing wrong with trying to present a pure, uncompromising ministry in a relevant and desirable format. Purity of message does not exempt us from our responsibility of relevance and quality. However, our attempts to be relevant and appealing should not dilute the message or compromise the values of the Gospel.

INTERNAL POSITIONING FOR CHURCHES

As in the illustration of the dog food company, we have all been lured to new businesses and restaurants based on their creative external positioning or marketing, only to be disappointed with the service, selection, quality, or organization we encountered. Typically in such cases, not only do we not return, but we warn other people about our experience. The same thing happens with ministries that invest in quality promotional materials and advertising while the ministry on the inside doesn't meet the expectations of the people who come. We must be able to deliver what we promise and promote.

While connecting the dots to determine a general shape or image can be challenging and fun, if we were required to connect the dots to create internal components of these shapes it would be much more complex. We can all agree it is one thing to connect the dots to draw the shape of a car or even a person, but if we had to draw the internal parts of an engine or a human body, we would need the capable help of engineers and scientists. The same is true of a ministry. **It is one thing to cast a vision or draw a picture of the future, but when it comes to the internal workings to make the vision come to pass, that requires another level of skill and experience.**

My connecting-the-dots attraction undoubtedly influenced my decision to enroll in a vocational technical school in high school to learn the art of drafting. From day one in my class, I was "connecting the dots." Over the course of two years, I learned how to plot the dots and then to connect them in order to create an accurate set of architectural drawings for a construction project or an engineering design that could be manufactured into a piece of equipment. The easy part was drawing the elevation of the building or the external shape of the equipment, which could typically be captured in a few pages. However, the detailed pages of each level of design and construction that had to take place to produce the image on the front involved weeks of work and multiple pages. Internal positioning is the equivalent to the detailed pages of the construction project or piece of equipment that is to be manufactured.

However, there are several things that are unique to a church or ministry that cannot be simply illustrated through the connect-the-dots imagery. Inside an organization there are not only the inanimate resources like buildings, equipment, and materials, there are also the human resources and intangible elements like vision and ministry, which must be properly positioned in relation to all of the other components.

In order to understand internal positioning, we will examine the various aspects of the following definition:

> *Internal positioning is "the manner in which a person or organization is arranged, aligned, equipped, strengthened, and brought into proper coordination and cooperation."*

It is necessary to break down this definition into individual "dots" that we will connect along the way. To the degree that we are able to connect these dots in a ministry, it will significantly determine the degree of internal positioning that is achievable. The failure to adequately connect the internal dots is typically the reason that a ministry may have a good flow of guests to their services and activities but a low level of return visits or retention.

ARRANGED: TO PUT IN PROPER ORDER, TO SORT SYSTEMATICALLY.

This aspect of internal positioning addresses the need for organization and order, specifically through the incorporation of systems. These systems include administrative, financial, assimilation, discipleship, and any other ministry systems that must be in place for effective ministry. Churches and ministries that lack a sufficient degree of organization and order, or effective and efficient systems for providing ministry to people when they arrive on their campus, not only demonstrate poor stewardship of the time, energy, and resources of people, but they also frustrate those who have come with a reasonable expectation that their needs and interest would be satisfied by their encounter.

I realize that, for some, my reference to "a healthy degree of organization and order, or effective systems" is too vague and ambiguous. **My intent is to recognize that there is significant diversity among the various organizational and ministry structures of churches (not to mention the diversity of worship styles).** Some churches may embrace a congregational form of government, while others prefer an elder led system or possibly engage in a pastor led/elder supported structure. Some churches may significantly delay the implementation of vital ministry as a result of multiple committees and processes, while churches without these committees and processes equally delay the implementation of vital ministry through indecision or the lack of a process for ministry implementation.

The emphasis on a "healthy degree of organization, order and systems" is to point out the importance of not allowing organization, order, or systems to interfere with the ability to effectively ministry to the needs of people in a timely and effective manner; nor do I recommend a lack of organization and order or the absence of systems and structures that produce the same result.

ALIGNED: TO BRING INTO A STRAIGHT LINE, PROCESS OR FLOW.

This dimension of internal positioning addresses the necessity of having all of the ministries, members (participants), money, and momentum moving in the same direction for a common cause or goal. Diversity is extremely important in meeting the various needs of people. However, unity and alignment in diversity is non-negotiable. As I pointed out earlier, when the Apostle Paul describes the church or the body of Christ, he indicated that we are many members, but we are one body. The effective mobility (momentum) of a human body is predicated upon the need for all of the members of the body to be properly aligned in order to have healthy mobility and function.

I personally enjoy the benefits of a skilled chiropractor. I am constantly amazed at how significant the proper alignment of the spine and skeletal frame is to the overall health and mobility of my body. I have watched in awe as the skillful hands of the chiropractor performed a mild and simple adjustment on an infant, which relieved the child of its colic condition. I have personally benefited from the adjustments to my spine that relieved pain and discomfort that seemed completely disassociated from my spine.

When the ministries, members (participants), money, and momentum within a church are not all properly aligned to bring forth a common vision, goal, or objective, then they actually impair the effectiveness of the other ministries in their contribution to the process. In such cases, the ministries, members (participants), money, and momentum of the church need to be realigned, so they can produce healthy mobility and function.

EQUIPPED: TO FURNISH WITH THE NECESSITIES FOR AN UNDERTAKING, TO PREPARE FOR SOME PARTICULAR DUTY OR SERVICE.

Internal positioning addresses the process of equipping and furnishing members and ministries with the skills, training, and resources needed to fulfill their specific assignment and purpose in the ministry. Nothing is more frustrating to ministry partners and leaders than to be asked to fulfill a specific assignment, only to be inadequately equipped, resourced, or furnished for the task.

In cases where there simply aren't enough resources for all of the ministries, then we must evaluate which ministries can and should be either temporarily or permanently suspended. Every ministry must identify its own critical mass—the point of maximum effectiveness which may be achieved through the utilization of the least amount of time, energy, and resources. In brief, it is the realization that "less (activity) can be more (productive)."

I am confident that within every church there are sufficient members and resources to fulfill the assignments and provide the ministries that the church should be engaged in—*at that time*. This doesn't always mean that the church should downsize to the level of volunteerism and giving that a church currently has. It may mean that the leadership of the church must find a more effective means of cultivating a greater level of involvement and investment by the congregation to fulfill the ministry assignments the church should fulfill. However, there must be an honest evaluation and realization that every church cannot do everything. Each church must honestly assess its stewardship capacity and potential and design a ministry structure that is based on this assessment.

> I am confident that within every church there are sufficient members and resources to fulfill the assignments and provide the ministries that the church should be engaged in—at that time.

Without question, when church leadership has an accurate assessment of their capacity and potential, they should design a ministry action plan that maximizes their ability, effectively equips their volunteers, and furnishes the resources needed for these ministries.

STRENGTHENED: TO MAKE STRONG OR STRONGER; TO ADD STRENGTH, TO ENCOURAGE, EMPOWER, TO GIVE THE CAPACITY FOR PRODUCING AN EFFECT OR RESULT.

When members and ministries lack sufficient strength—emotionally, spiritually, skillfully, and relationally—they will not be healthy enough to produce the ministry result that is desired or intended. Internal positioning develops and implements an intentional system for the strength and health of its members and ministries.

Many churches report a significant decline or dropout of volunteers in ministry. When asked the reason given by those withdrawing from involvement, the typical response is burnout or weariness. In the face of this reality, churches must realize that the antidote for burnout and weariness is appreciation, encouragement, proper gift identification, and temporary relief.

In many places, when someone volunteers for ministry it is the equivalent of a life sentence without the possibility of parole. Many people have responded to the need for volunteers by saying, "I'll do it until you can find someone else," only to find themselves seemingly trapped in an assignment permanently. Unfortunately, many of these people believe the only way out of this ministry assignment (life sentence) is to leave the church.

Every ministry must have an intentional plan of appreciation and encouragement. How many times have we witnessed an exhausted sports team rise with new energy as the crowd applauded, cheered, and encouraged them? Every church should have a weekly, monthly, quarterly, and annual plan for appreciation and encouragement to those who are serving in ministry.

Many people who seem to lack the strength of effectiveness in an area of ministry may simply be serving in the wrong area of ministry. Every ministry should have a strategy and system for identifying the unique spiritual gifts, interest, desires, burdens, and passions of individuals who are willing to serve and place them within those areas. An individual that is gifted to work with children may look "weak" when asked to sing or play an instrument; but when they are with children they excel! A person who seems frustrated or weak in a particular area of ministry may simply be in the wrong area of ministry. Internal positioning involves interviewing and assessing the ministry giftedness of these individuals and placing them in an appropriate area of ministry.

One of the most significant things a ministry can do to extend the longevity of service from their gifted volunteers is to offer to give them a brief time off—without making them feel guilty. I have discovered that giving someone a couple of weeks off from their responsibilities and providing them the opportunity to receive the ministry of the Word in the worship services, small groups, or fellowship groups without being pulled away by other responsibilities can be spiritually, emotionally, and physically refreshing and rejuvenating.

COORDINATION: THE PROCESS OF RESOURCES AND PROCESSES WORKING TOGETHER IN HARMONY, UNITY AND WITH NECESSARY FLEXIBILITY TO ACHIEVE A COMMON PURPOSE OR GOAL.

One of the most significant areas of internal positioning is the coordination of resources and processes, the systems and structures of the ministry. The resources here refer to the facility and equipment available to the church. The processes refer to the schedules, ministry systems, and approval processes of the church. Many ministries are limited in their effectiveness and undermined in their potential because of territorialism involving space and equipment. Equally damaging is the unwillingness to coordinate ministry schedules or perhaps the failure to submit timely request for approval.

Internal positioning dedicates the necessary time to develop, implement, and maintain effective systems and structures to coordinate access and approval needed for effective ministry. This often requires regularly scheduled meetings of staff and volunteer ministry leaders to review calendars, facility needs, equipment requests, and ministry event approval. In addition, a system for submitting requests for approval between these scheduled meetings should be established.

The coordination of systems and structures also includes the integration and communication that must exist between the various ministries and systems of the church such as the administrative systems, assimilation ministries, and discipleship or spiritual formation ministries.

COOPERATION: THE PROCESS OF A GROUP OF PEOPLE WORKING TOGETHER IN HARMONY, UNITY AND WITH NECESSARY FLEXIBILITY TO ACHIEVE A COMMON PURPOSE OR GOAL.

Perhaps the most challenging part of internal positioning is the portion that involves the cooperation of groups of people. In many aspects of internal positioning, the process involves working one-on-one with individuals who are involved in ministry. However, there still remains the process of leading groups of people to work together in harmony, unity, and with necessary flexibility to achieve a common purpose or goal.

One of the strategic keys to accomplishing this objective is to have a simple and concise mission statement or declaration that defines the church or ministry's reason for being. Most organizations suffer from *mission drift*. They have lost sight of their reason for being and therefore other issues become elevated to a disproportionate level of significance and importance.

Coupled with a simple and concise mission statement, there must be a clear and compelling vision. This vision must create a mental picture of a compelling and desired future that is embraced by those involved. It is possible for a group of people to know their reason for being but lack clarity about how they are to fulfill their mission, or for there to be a lack of compelling desire to see the vision come to pass. In other words, we must provide the numerical assignment or prioritized system of ministry that will allow the church to connect the dots.

> Only about twenty percent have an agreed vision statement that is customized, clear, and compelling.

In my time working with churches and conducting assessments I have discovered that about sixty percent of the churches have an agreed written mission statement. Only about twenty percent have an agreed vision statement that is customized, clear, and compelling. Less than ten percent have a strategic plan for implementing their mission and vision. One of the fundamental keys to leading people is to help them understand their reason for being and then to embrace a clear and compelling vision of what their mission will look like when it is fulfilled through their local ministry.

Mission and vision must be the unifying elements that bring people together in cooperation to fulfill a common purpose or goal. The absence of a clear and compelling vision gives an unspoken license to each person to create their own vision and to chart their own course, making cooperation impossible and creating a feeble system of co-existence at best.

CHAPTER FOUR

POSITIONING YOUR CHURCH WITHIN SEVEN CRITICAL ENVIRONMENTS

I have discovered that positioning must occur within seven internal and external *healthy environments* in which the people, resources, and processes function. An environment can be described in a variety of ways, depending on its application. As it relates to positioning your church, it can be defined as "the area or surroundings in which the ministry exists and operates."

Early in my marriage to my wife Robin, I learned just how critical a healthy environment is. My education came as a result of Robin's love for and gifted ability in creating a relaxing home environment filled with beautiful plants. I now know that Robin is not just gifted, she is wise in understanding the importance of the right environment for plants. My lack of understanding about the importance of the right environment for plants at this early stage would produce a great opportunity for me to acquire a valuable education.

My learning opportunity came at a time when Robin had to be away for a few days. Her final instructions to me before saying goodbye were, "Whatever you do, don't let the plants die." After a few days, I noticed the leaves on the plants were limping. Recalling the times when I witnessed her watering the plants, I decided to give them water. I was pleased the next day to see the plants responding to the water, so I decided to keep giving them water each day. You guessed it—this caused the plants to receive too much water, and they began to limp again.

After exercising my lifeline to "call a friend," I stopped watering the plants every day and moved the plants near the window to benefit from the indirect sunlight where they began to dry out. The next day, I saw the immediate benefits of putting the plants in the indirect sunlight, so I construed that they could potentially benefit even more by drying out in the direct sunlight. I moved the plants to the back porch only to discover that too much of a good thing (water or sun) will negatively impact an otherwise healthy plant.

> God has put "the ability to grow" in the DNA of every church! Churches simply do things, often within the various environments of the church, that prevents or hinders the ministry from growing.

I didn't have any lifelines left, so I took the initiative to move the plants indoors with a balance of indirect sunlight and periodic watering. Somehow I was successful in not killing the plants and upon her return they were in reasonably good condition.

Beyond the lesson I learned about the plants, I also learned that churches, like plants are generally healthy by God's design. In fact, I've learned that just as God has put in every plant's DNA the ability to grow, *God has also put the ability to grow in the DNA of every church*! We simply do things that prevent or hinder the church from growing. Simply stated, we often do things to churches (like plants) that affect their ability to grow. Specifically, we often create unhealthy environments that impair the growth potential of the church.

Throughout my years of providing church consulting or navigational services, I have been challenged on many occasions regarding my conclusion that God has placed "the ability to grow" in the DNA of every church. However, when given the opportunity to work with these churches and ministries, it has been confirmed repeatedly. We simply have to acknowledge that healthy churches are growing churches. If we can address the health issues (which often are internal) we can restore the church to health and growth.

Positioning your church requires identifying the seven critical environments that affect the health and growth of the church and then working to create a healthy environment within each area. To the degree that we can position the church in these seven healthy environments (just as I finally put the plants in the right environment) we can expect churches to be healthy and growing.

CREATING A HEALTHY
SPIRITUAL ENVIRONMENT

The first and most significant environment is the *spiritual* health environment in which the church is positioned. The experiences I have had in the places where I have personally served and in those that I have served as a consultant/coach/navigator have caused me to understand the importance of creating a healthy spiritual environment more than any other experience.

One of the ministries that I had the privilege of serving had experienced a variety of spiritual setbacks, including the departure of two senior pastors in two years, which was made more severe by the ending of their marriages shortly after their departures. During these previous two pastors there had also been the abrupt closing of the large Christian school that was hosted at the church, just a few weeks before opening of classes. This resulted in the church having responsibility to fulfil the financial responsibility of teacher contracts, as well as negative publicity by the media, which scrutinized the church for their poor timing in closing the school.

In addition to these negative experiences, there were several other situations that had taken place including the departure of many families—especially many young families. The church had also experienced a sharp drop in attendance from over 2,000 to only 300 within a two-year period, along with an equally devastating drop in finances. In addition, several charter members and mainstay members passed away within a short period of time. Without question there was a stronger sense of spiritual losses than spiritual wins or victories.

All of these factors took a significant toll on the spiritual environment of the congregation. Spiritual weariness, discouragement, disillusionment, and frustration had significantly diminished (if not completely stolen) the faith, courage, confidence, passion, and enthusiasm of the people. The most descriptive term that I could use to describe the people within the church was "spiritually traumatized and wounded."

As I spent extensive periods of time in prayer, seeking the guidance of the Holy Spirit, I received something from the Lord that enabled me to put a handle on my assignment of leading the church forward. What I received I'm hesitant to call a vision from God, because I don't want to suggest that I should be privileged to receive a divine vision from God, nor do I want some to dismiss the significance of what I received because of the identification I give to you. **Whether it was a vision, a dream, or simply an impression, without question it was an illustration to show me what to do in this situation.**

In this illustration, I received a phone call informing me that a young couple that I had recently performed a wedding ceremony for had been involved in a life-threatening car accident. In the illustration they had been rushed to the emergency room at a nearby hospital awaiting imminent life-saving surgeries.

As I viewed myself driving to the emergency room, I was contemplating what I would say to this young couple to give them courage and hope in the face of this devastating accident. I quickly dismissed the idea of asking them distracting questions about their future such as: "Have you been looking for your dream home?"; or "Have you thought about having children yet?"; or "Have you picked out the names of your future children?"; or "Have you set up college funds for your children and thought about where they will attend school some day?" This difficult moment could not be adequately addressed through a series of distracting efforts. There needed to be careful and compassionate confrontation of the current reality that provided courage and confidence.

I dismissed these ridiculous questions because I knew that at the present moment they couldn't think about the future; they were fighting for survival. They were facing emergency life-saving surgeries. What they needed at the present moment was support for their faith and prayer for courage to go through this process. With that in mind, I began imagining myself praying for God's divine favor and intervention in their situation. I began telling them that God had given these doctors the skills they needed for this very situation and that the Lord's presence would be with them in that surgery room.

The illustration continued to unfold in my mind and I saw them coming out of emergency surgery and being taken to the intensive care unit where they would stay for an undetermined number of days until they were stable enough to be transferred to a general hospital room. A few days later they were transferred to the regular hospital room where they were told that they would have to go through physical therapy and rehabilitation for several months before they could be released from the hospital and be able to return to their jobs and lives again.

Finally, in the illustration that was unfolding in my mind, I was there when the doctors gave them the release from rehabilitation and they were going home for the first time. They had a much different look on their faces than when I first saw them in the emergency room, when they were fighting for their lives. Now the fear had been replaced with faith and uncertainty had been replaced with confidence. Now they were ready to pick up their lives and move forward.

As I reviewed this illustration repeatedly in my mind and in my prayers, the Holy Spirit impressed upon me that the young couple represented the church congregation I was trying to lead forward with vision, outreach, and church growth. The reason the church wasn't responding and the church wasn't growing was because, just like that young couple, they were traumatized and wounded and fighting for survival—not physically, but spiritually. They were spiritually traumatized and wounded. They were fighting for their spiritual survival.

The Holy Spirit then impressed upon me that my role at the present moment was to first lead the congregation from this place of spiritual

trauma to a place of spiritual restoration. This would involve walking with them through emergency surgery, a time of intensive care, and eventually to a place where they can be transferred spiritually to a regular room. After a time to build their strength, they would go through rehabilitation and spiritual therapy so they could spiritually walk again and eventually be released back into Christian service. Any attempts to preach about vision or the future of the ministry would at best be a diversion from the trauma, but it would not address the trauma they were experiencing.

Finally in the illustration, I was able to share the vision, dreams, and plans for the ministry, and they were able to embrace them with faith and courage again. In the case of this church I was serving, the healing process took approximately seven years. However, when it was complete I knew it. Everyone knew it! There was a complete change in the spiritual environment of the church. We were ready to become more fully engaged in ministry to reaching out to the unbelievers and embracing new believers. What had seemed hopeless and unachievable in the first seven years was now being accomplished in months.

> There are specific factors that determine the turnaround timeframe.

I don't want to suggest that every church will require seven years before it will experience a turnaround, but that was the time needed for this particular church. I have discovered that there are specific factors that determine the turnaround timeframe. Things such as the age of the church, how recent the trauma was experienced, the size of the church before and after the most recent decline or traumatic experience, the experience and the gifting of the pastor, and many other factors all impact the time required for a complete and successful turnaround process.

When I look back over that experience, I see the same thing happening in many churches today. New pastors arrive at their new place of ministry, excited and ready to share their ministry vision and dreams of the future, only to find that the congregation doesn't share the same level of passion or excitement. However, it's not because they don't want to. It's because they can't. Often times they have been spiritually traumatized or wounded and they need a time of healing.

One of the first assignments of a pastor who arrives at a traumatized church should be to focus on creating a healthy spiritual environment. Share messages of hope, faith and encouragement. Slow down and minister to their spiritual wounds, disappointments and disillusionments. If the pastor will take the time to walk the congregation through a time of spiritual healing and renewal, when they experience their spiritual healing they will stand with him and support him in the fulfilling of the vision God has given to him. I know! The congregations I have been personally involved with did it for me and with me.

CREATING A HEALTHY EMOTIONAL ENVIRONMENT

It is very likely that the second environment that must be addressed is the emotional environment. Much like the spiritual environment, the congregation may have been emotionally traumatized and wounded. However, instead of struggling with God and their faith, people typically struggle emotionally as result of their experiences with other people.

It has been my experience that the most significant trauma typically comes from the feeling of emotional betrayal. Just saying the word betrayal undoubtedly stirs memories of your own past experiences, or perhaps your present experience.

It may be that the experience of betrayal affects us more emotionally than any other experience. When a spouse discovers that his mate has betrayed their love through an affair with another person, the sting of betrayal engulfs his emotions. When someone you have personally helped, maybe even rescued from perhaps more than one situation, turns against you and not only speaks evil about you, but even shares the confidences that you had shared, you feel the sting of betrayal. Or perhaps when you have put a high level of trust and confidence in a person, only to discover they have deceived you, betrayed your trust, and taken advantage of you.

For the congregation and church that I previously mentioned, there was an unhealthy emotional environment. Most of this emotional trauma seemed to come from two sources. First, there was emotional trauma that came from seeing their pastors' marriages end in divorce after a very short time from their departure. Admittedly, in both cases, most of the people who were in leadership were already aware of the personal strain that was upon their pastor's marriages. Those who were aware of the troubled marriages of their leaders passionately prayed that God would sustain their marriages. When their marriages fell apart, some felt betrayed by leaders who had insisted that divorce should be avoided at all cost and God could save marriages if family members would pray and ask for His divine intervention. I encountered many people who felt like they were betrayed, being told to stick it out in their own difficult marriages, only to see their pastors seemingly take the easy way out. Now these congregational members had stayed in their difficult marriages, but those they trusted had ended theirs.

My words to these betrayed hearts seem to fall on deaf ears. Many times I tried to point out that the enemy seems to fight the marriages of leaders harder than others, knowing that if he can disrupt their marriages it will impact many others, just as it had done—leaving them feeling betrayed and lied to. They had put their trust and confidence in the reassuring words and Biblical counsel of their leaders, only for them to seemingly respond otherwise.

A second source of betrayal was from all of the close friends and fellow believers who had left the church at some point during the departure and transition of these two previous pastors. This side of betrayal seemed to be based on a feeling of resentment. On one hand, those who stayed probably wished they had been released by God to walk away from all that was crumbling around them. However, feeling no release, they were committed to weathering the storm—no matter how long it lasted. Their personal conviction about their decision to stay at the church didn't prevent them from feeling betrayed by the departing people whom they had prayed with and for, worshipped with, and served beside. They often found themselves asking, "Where are the people we fellowshipped with in their homes and ours?"

Much of this sense of betrayal was rooted in the fact that they questioned whether the people who left had even prayed about their decision. They seriously doubted that God would tell everyone to "abandon ship," leaving the ministry more weakened and more vulnerable than it already was by the departures of their pastors and their dissolving marriages. Further adding to their sense of betrayal was the increased financial weight of the ministry that fell on the shoulders of those who stayed. Instead of being able to walk away and enjoy the opportunity to worship in a healthy congregation, they felt betrayed and rejected by those they had counted on to stick with them through the good times and bad times.

My responsibility as the pastor was made much more difficult not only by the departure of most of the congregation and increased financial weight on the few, but by three additional factors. **First, I was responsible for rebuilding the trust and confidence that had been broken by the previous pastors.** For the first five years that Robin and I were at this church, people regularly approached me asking if our marriage was okay. We were repeatedly questioned about whether or not we needed to go away to a marriage enrichment opportunity. The congregation was suspicious of the sincerity of our love and commitment to each other. Could they really trust what we were saying publicly? What was really going on behind closed doors?

Secondly, my task was made more difficult because the existing members of the congregation were suspicious of the small remnant that remained and possibly resistant to the idea of those who had left potentially returning in the future. They questioned who would be next to abandon them and leave. Even if someone insisted on their commitment to stay and support the church and see it restored to new strength, those who remained could not fully invest their trust in their words, having been betrayed by others they thought would have never left. Those who remained also struggled with their emotions regarding those who might potentially return after the church reached a new level of strength and health.

Thirdly, I found myself being held in suspicion of potentially betraying both the remaining staff members and their family members that were still in the congregation. The reason for their suspicion was simply based on the fact that most of the staff was still in place from the time when the church was running well over 2,000 on Sunday mornings. Through the transitions, those in temporary leadership tried to avoid releasing staff members or terminating employees, anticipating that it would further escalate the departure of the family members and friends relationally connected to these staff members. Of course their anticipation of additional departures was correct.

When I informed the staff that I would be taking the first six months to evaluate the roles and effectiveness of each staff member along with the church's ability to financially retain staff, a spirit of betrayal arose. These staff members had in fact stayed through the storm. Few, if any had mailed out their resumes to look for other places of employment. Some did not seek out other employment because they did not want their departure to further impact the church. Undoubtedly, some did not seek other employment because they wanted to stay and see the church return to new strength and viability. Now, I was announcing that employment cuts were unavoidable and they felt betrayed. Likewise, the family members and friends of those that were eventually released also felt betrayed and left the church when the staff member's employment ended.

What do you do when both the congregation and the remaining staff members feel betrayed? You do the only thing you can do. You continue to reassure people that your marriage is fine, to encourage them to pray for those who left trying to spiritually survive and yet might return, as well as their personal attitudes toward them. In addition, those who felt betrayed by having their employment ended had to remove their emotions from the situation and understand the pure economic situation. Few understood. Most needed time to heal and trust again. So, while we were actively restoring a healthy spiritual environment, we were also working to restore trust and confidence.

Many pastors arrive at churches where the previous pastor may have been engaged in a moral failure, a marriage failure, ministry failure, lack of success, or perhaps the pastor kept telling the people that he wanted to be their pastor until he died—while all the time he was circulating his resume for another church. **These new pastors must realize that**

although someone else created the sense of betrayal, for a season, people will incorrectly transfer that emotional mistrust to them.

New leaders must diligently work from day one to rebuild people's ability to trust. It is not because the new leaders are untrustworthy that the congregation struggles; it is because they feel betrayed. New leaders should not make promises they can't keep and they should not try to over compensate for the struggles of the congregation by trying to create a premature

> New leaders must diligently work from day one to rebuild people's ability to trust.

environment of trust. Give them time. Pray for them and love them through their struggle. They will come around. I know! The churches I have led through their emotional struggle of betrayal eventually gave me their complete trust and support!

CREATING A HEALTHY RELATIONAL ENVIRONMENT

When churches are not reaching their potential in ministry, the current relational environment of the church can either be considered a contributing factor or a part of the collateral damage. Often times an unhealthy relational environment may have started out being a contributing factor only to see the challenge of internal relationships to be further strained by their experiences.

UNMET EXPECTATIONS

Unmet expectations often create an unhealthy relational environment. When expectations are not being met, frustration flourishes. I have often said that frustration is often vented either to those we have the deepest relationship with or with whomever is around us at the moment. The undeniable truth is that **personal frustration affects the relational environment in which people find themselves.** When frustration arises from unmet expectations within a church it affects the internal relationships. These strained relationships may exist between any and all of the various people within the congregation including the pastor, congregation, church leadership, staff members, and ministry volunteers. The possibility for any number of strained relationships is almost endless.

The strain in these relationships is the result of trying to identify whom to blame for the unmet ministry expectations. The pastor may feel the congregation is not supporting his or her vision, or possibly that a staff member is not fully investing themselves in the vision and goals that have been established. The congregation may feel that the pastor is not leading effectively, or that a governing board is acting too passively about the critical decisions affecting the ministry. Ultimately, unmet ministry expectations typically evolve into a blame game, trying to *assign* responsibility rather than *accept* responsibility.

Just as children in a household can sense when there is a strained relationship between the parents, even if they did not witness an argument or confrontation, the same is true by those who attend the church, and especially by those who may visit the church. **When the congregation senses or is a part of a strained relationship within the church, one of the first things they stop doing is inviting new people to the church.** No one wants to invite new people into an unstable or possibly even a hostile environment, unless they believe that the individuals they have invited have the potential to help. When new people visit the church, they can almost immediately sense the relational tension that exists and it affects their overall experience. As a result of this tense or unstable environment they are not likely to return. New people are the key to reaching a ministry's potential. Therefore, when the congregation *shuts down* relationally, the lifeline of new growth is shut down as well.

POWER STRUGGLES

Power struggles are another contributing factor to an unhealthy church environment. I have encountered some congregations where there seemed to be some form of standoff going on between the pastor and congregation, pastor and board, board and congregation, or possibly even between different groups within the congregation. The standoff was either the result of some strong-willed person or persons who refused to cooperate with the will of the larger group, or perhaps it was a significant decision that was being considered by the congregation. Ultimately, these unhealthy relational environments will almost always result in someone or a specific group of people leaving the ministry, possibly further weakening the ministry as a whole.

In most power struggles, the significant question is, "Who will have the most influence in the decisions and directions of the ministry?" Those who have been a part of the church for an extended period of time may feel they should have a greater voice or influence. Individuals in leadership may feel threatened by the arrival of new people, concerned that they may be replaced by "new blood." Others who have been significant financial contributors may feel that the size of their giving should determine the size of their vote or influence. When all is said and done, power struggles exist because someone (not everyone) is more interested in imposing their will or preferences in a disproportionate level on the direction and decisions that are being made for the ministry.

I have long contended that when people's ideas and insights are determined to be the most beneficial for the ministry, the congregation readily embraces them. I also believe that if someone new became a part of the congregation with fresh ideas and insights it would help the congregation not only receive an honest assessment of their ministry, but also provide them with a new perspective for ministry. For these and many other reasons, these new individuals should be embraced and not shunned. However, there are unfortunately those who are more influenced by their need to protect their position than to advance the kingdom of God.

I've definitely had my share of experiences with power struggles. I grew up in a church in which I had seventeen pastors in fifteen years and all of these were during my formative years. As a young child, I watched the tears flow down the faces of the congregation at the departure of yet another pastor, while a climate of hope surrounded the arrival of the incoming pastor. Through those pastoral transitions, I noticed that if the church didn't grow, then the pastor was often "encouraged" to leave. However, if the church began to grow under the leadership of a new pastor, the arrival of the new people or "new blood" immediately began to threaten the positions of existing leadership. The only solution the existing or established members had in order to preserve their positions of influence was to either "encourage" another pastor to leave or to "encourage" the new people to leave.

Having become experienced in this "ministry of encouragement," they knew that if they only encouraged the new people to leave, that it would only be a matter of time until the pastor was able to reach more new people. However, if they encouraged the pastor to leave, it would eliminate both the immediate and future threat to their positions. In such cases, their encouragement to the pastor typically came in the form of withholding the financial support that was necessary to support the pastor and his family. On more than one occasion I heard the strategy repeated: "If he won't leave, we'll starve him out."

> It's amazing to me how people will fight to preserve the little perceived power of influence they can have among thirty-five people

In my first opportunity to lead a congregation, although I had witnessed these power struggles many times, I was so optimistic that it wouldn't happen to me that I was blind-sided by the first power struggle that manifested. The church I was called to lead was over seventy-five years old, in a neighborhood that had experienced such a significant demographic shift the area was no longer considered a white, middle-class community, but it had been tagged as "Hell's forty acres." The composition of the neighborhood had resulted in congregational "white flight," except for the older senior adults who simply couldn't afford to relocate or refused to drive to a church in a different neighborhood.

Through a series of unfortunate pastoral transitions, the church that I had once been a guest evangelist in when it had over three hundred in attendance, had now fallen to an attendance of thirty-five over a period of a few short years. It's amazing to me how people will fight to preserve the little perceived power of influence they can have among thirty-five people, knowing that at least a third of the congregational members are usually related to them. Nevertheless, after leading the church to about seventy people within six months we encountered our first head-to-head power struggle.

In the absence of a significant number of people in general, we also had an insignificant number of what our constitution and bylaws deemed "qualified individuals" to serve on the church leadership team. In view of this dilemma and yet wanting to preserve the qualifications for office that were obviously highly valued and embraced by those who were currently in elected office, I chose to exercise my prerogative of appointing special leadership teams and task forces. In essence, I created a parallel leadership group, which I called the Church Growth Council.

While the members of this group had no official vote, they could make recommendations to the congregation and church leadership for consideration. As newly arriving people were quickly outnumbering the established people, the potential of a "congregational or leadership override" was clearly in view. You guessed it. A "power move" was now viewed as necessary in order to preserve and protect their ministry influence over thirty-five people.

To the disadvantage of the existing group who had actually called me to this place of ministry, my prior experience of seventeen pastors in fifteen years and their various "starve the pastor" coups had prepared me for this conflict. At the risk of losing either the established crowd or the arriving crowd, I simply revealed what I felt was the heart of the issue. I addressed the perception of the established crowd being pushed aside as the new individuals were coming in. Those who failed to acknowledge their insecurity and hidden personal agenda, left abruptly, while those who had just arrived and did not have a personal agenda were stunned to discover that their enthusiasm and willingness to come alongside a struggling ministry had been interpreted as some form of "ministry takeover."

The existence and operation of power struggles are not limited to the smaller churches. When I arrived at a much larger place of ministry, there was a clearly established group of influencers, which had been in decision-making leadership roles for an extended period of time. Their longevity had been perpetuated by the absence of any form of term limits or board member rotation. The average tenure on the board was over fourteen years when I arrived. Newer board members seemed more open to embrace new ideas, while the more established members often seemed to me to be more interested in preserving their positions.

I was still relatively young when I arrived to this particular pastorate (thirty-three years of age). Undoubtedly some of the established members may have viewed me as being a person that they could direct with their decision-making authority. Of course, the more established members insisted their decisions and

The pastor must be viewed as the spiritual head of the church.

"encouragements" were based on the fact that they had been here longer than I had (and even longer than the newer board members) and they knew best. However, my experience in leading a previous turnaround church, followed by an effective church planting experience, caused me to believe there were decisions that needed to be made for growth that were going to be uncomfortable for some of the elected decision-makers.

One of the decisions that I presented to the congregation was to establish term limits on elected decision-makers, thereby implementing a board rotation and allowing the opportunity for new people with new ideas and insights to be included in the decision-making process. Of course, this congregation had become primarily a board-led congregation during their two difficult pastoral transitions. During the long absences without a pastor, the church board had become the primary decision-makers and they enjoyed the role. Relinquishing the leadership of the church to a new pastor or to new people was not going to be easy.

At my first board meeting at this particular church, I was informed that I was the pastor, but someone else was the chairman of the board. Fortunately, the constitution and bylaws of the church clearly stated that when a new pastor was selected, he would assume the role as chairman of the board. I realize there are churches that may operate under a system in which the pastor is not the chairman of the board. However, even in these situations, the pastor must be viewed as the spiritual head of the church, with the chairman and other board members understanding their role of supporting the vision set forth by the pastor and to serve with the purpose of facilitating the necessary resources to fulfill the vision, not competing with the pastor for leadership and influence in the congregation. **I prefer to identify this arrangement as a "Pastor led, board/elder supportive" system.**

Needless to say, the established board members didn't like the idea of term limits and a rotational board, even though I assured each of them that if they were in fact actively involved in the life and ministry of the church and the congregation that they would most likely be returned to office after a one year break in service. What took place next was a clear confirmation that the congregation's support for term limits (two three-year terms, followed by one year off before being eligible to return) was in fact one of the healthiest decisions that was made in this critical time.

Those who seemed to only find their significance or value in an elected position, left as soon as their term expired. They blew their cover! Everyone knew immediately that they were only going to attend the church if they were one of the "decision-makers." If they couldn't be decision-makers, they would leave—and they did.

Not all of the elected decision-makers left when their terms expired. About one-third of those who faced term limits remained active in the life and ministry of the church, and when they were eligible to return to an elected leadership role, they were invited by the congregation to do so. These individuals not only gained significant respect by me, they gained significant respect from the entire congregation, because they stayed when others left.

TERRITORIALISM

Territorialism is another element that creates an unhealthy relational environment. This occurs when adults revert back to their early childhood emotionally, unwilling to share their space or their resources. In many of these places, getting permission to use a particular space or resource that has been historically associated with a particular ministry is in fact like taking candy from a baby. You may get it, but someone will be screaming, unless you offer a sufficient exchange that will cause the child (or adult) to cooperate.

One of my first encounters with territorialism occurred when I borrowed a music stand as a temporary speaker's podium so I could move closer to the reduced congregation in a large auditorium. After the service, I was quickly notified that the music stand belonged to the music department and that people (including me) were not supposed to move the music stands from the platform for any reason. Being new to the ministry, I made a mental note (or so I thought) and planned to visit a local store where I could purchase a simple wood podium for the next week. However, somehow I forgot to get the wood podium, and so I made the mistake of thinking it would be okay to use the music stand for one more week. When I went to get the music stand, I discovered that someone had taken a bottle of liquid white out and painted a large message which stated: "For Music Ministry Only, Do Not Remove!" Although it didn't say it in large print, I was quite sure that in small print it probably said "and this includes you pastor!"

I cannot be sure of the actual percentage of my time that I have spent separating squabbling children—I mean church people—and resolving conflicts that had at the core the issue of territorialism. Believe me, I understand that **people should have the reasonable expectation that the space and resources which have been secured for the purpose of enabling them to fulfill their ministry should be available and in good condition when they need them.**

The effectiveness of the overall ministry of the church is significantly dependent upon the various ministries of the church understanding that we are all on the same team.

I fully understand that the midweek children's ministry group shouldn't consume all of the children's snacks that they discovered in the storage cabinet as though this was divinely placed there like manna from heaven, without a sense of responsibility to replace or arrange for the replacement of snacks before the Sunday children's ministry group arrives. I fully understand the frustration of arriving on Sunday with the worship team ready to lead worship, only to find pieces of the musical equipment or microphones have been "borrowed" by another ministry but never returned or possibly returned, but broken. I have lived through all of these experiences and many more. However, territorialism is not the solution to these challenges, teamwork is!

The antidote for territorialism is leading people into understanding that they are actually all on the same team and that teamwork will

always produce a better result that territorialism. We are, after all, all on the same ministry team. The effectiveness of the overall ministry of the church is significantly dependent upon the various ministries of the church understanding that we are all on the same team. If one ministry area has a space or resource that can better serve another ministry group (especially if it is a growing ministry group), those currently using the space or resource should be willing to relocate temporarily or even permanently to accommodate the new or growing ministry group's needs.

INGROWN RELATIONSHIPS

Ingrown relationships can be another challenge that the congregation will have to address. Many churches believe they are friendly, but they are only friendly to themselves. We also must realize that there is a difference between being friendly and being relational. Shaking hands and presenting smiling faces, possibly coupled with a kind greeting or brief assistance in finding a location, is not the same as being relational. Being relational involves being open and intentional about developing new relationships with new people.

Assimilation of new people requires an intentional plan for developing new relationships. Studies vary on the exact number of new relationships or time frame with which to achieve the assimilation of new people, but the most common references seem to indicate that a new person coming to a church must develop at least six new friends in six months or they most likely will move on.

Relationships are the glue that not only increase the retention of new people within a church, but also keep volunteers in ministries. People don't want to simply help a church or ministry fulfill its vision or goals without having the benefit of relationships. Healthy relationships are needed not only because they provide a sense of belonging, but because they create an environment for personal rejuvenation. We are refreshed by our friends. While we work alongside others in a ministry project, we should benefit, as much if not more so, through our service because of the relationship factor. People don't want to feel used or taken advantage of; they want to feel "a part of." Specifically, they want to feel like they are a part of you and your life.

People are not looking for more busy activity in their life. There is more than enough busy activity already. People are searching for genuine, meaningful, and fulfilling relationships. When churches are so ingrown that they only fellowship with their existing group or simply don't have room in their relational circles to include others, the church will be unable to assimilate new people. This is the logic behind starting new small groups or having existing small groups restart on a regular basis in order to welcome new people. New people won't force their way into closed societies, but they will make their way into open communities.

> The relational environment of the congregation will have profound impact on the growth or decline of a local ministry.

In the final analysis, the relational environment of the congregation will have profound impact on the growth or decline of a local ministry. Regardless of how a congregation perceives itself, having the benefit of an outsider, whether an experienced secret church "shopper" or worshipper or simply asking a fellow pastor to "member swap" for a Sunday — selecting individuals to visit each other's churches and to share their experiences — is a beneficial tool for gauging the "relational environment" of the church.

CREATING A HEALTHY PHYSICAL (FACILITY) ENVIRONMENT

Without question, one of the most observed *environments* that people are aware of in the church is the facility or physical environment. While much has been written about the physical environment of the church, our observations would not be complete without addressing this critical area. The undeniable reality is that we are very visual people. First impressions do matter. We never get a second chance to make a first impression.

At one of the places in which I served, while most people may have been awestruck by the size and location of the facility, I was immediately calculating the cost of repairs, enhancements, maintenance, and relevant expansion that would eventually be needed. This was further driven home a couple of years after my arrival. I was engaged in a conversation with a woman who had recently become a part of the local congregation. I asked her more about her journey to the church and how it came about.

Her story further galvanized my strong conviction that appearance does matter. She told me that she had actually felt impressed to visit the church about one year earlier. However, when she pulled in from the main road, she immediately saw things that raised serious concerns in her mind. She saw the poor condition of the parking lot, pieces of the roofing materials that were missing, portions of the wood siding that were either missing or falling, and many other things that she detailed for me as my heart continued to sink. Then she made a statement that has remained with me: "When I saw the condition of the church, I said to the Lord, if they can't take care of their buildings and property, how are they going to take care of me?"

What she didn't know when she pulled into our church parking lot and then pulled out before attending a service was that we were working behind the scenes to address all of the concerns she had shared with me. However, as someone who just pulled in and pulled away, she had no idea that we were even trying to do something with our facility. That's why many construction sites put up large billboards or banners showing

First impressions do matter.

the future result of their efforts. They want to send a message to people that they are "a work in progress." The same is true of the church. People want to see progress, and they are willing to stay if they at least see that there is a work in progress.

In my personal research, I have discovered that the fastest growing segment of growth in churches today is among young families. Without going into detail as to why new growth is coming from this segment, we should instead focus on what it will require in order to retain the harvest of young families that are making their way into churches.

- First and foremost, we must acknowledge the fact that young families are choosing churches for their children in the same way they are choosing schools and neighborhoods to live in. Young families view these choices as "quality of life" decisions, and they are committed to doing everything in their power to give their children a better quality of life than perhaps the one they experienced for themselves.

- In considering this new growth segment in the local church, we have discovered that young families want to take their children to a ministry in which the quality of the children's area and overall ministry is equal to or better than the home and neighborhood in which they live. Seldom will you find a family taking their children to a church in which the quality of the facility or the ministry area is of a lower quality than their home and neighborhood. This requires every church to thoroughly examine its existing nursery and children's ministry areas to determine if they meet or exceed the expectations of these young families.

- Another way to determine if the church is meeting these expectations is to visit the nursery and children's ministry areas of various growing churches, especially those with the closest proximity to the church. There will undoubtedly be those who argue that if the nursery and children's ministry areas were good enough for their children, it should be good enough for the next generation of children. That's the problem! It's the *good enough* perspective. If it was good enough for me, it should be good enough for them. Cars without air conditioning were good enough for people years ago, but it's not the acceptable standard for today. At one time churches had no type of padded seating in their worship areas, but today you will be hard pressed to find a church without padded seating. We can't let *good enough* be our standard if we want to create a healthy physical environment for ministry.

First impressions do matter, especially in terms of facilities. I've heard it stated that most people will decide in the first seven minutes they are at a church, whether or not they will return. The first seven minutes usually takes place before they hear a worship song, much less a sermon. Those first seven minutes are typically associated with the church facility. It begins at the entrance to your church with curb appeal, access, and external signage. But it continues inside to facility entrances, nursery and children's areas, restrooms, and then the worship area itself.

> Most people will decide in the first seven minutes they are at a church, whether or not they will return.

We all realize that facility maintenance is an ongoing challenge; and if you are in a rented facility, there are limitations that you must contend with. In these cases, create an informative resource with color pictures and images of the environment you are working towards. Your communication may introduce your future facility enhancements, a relocation to a different facility, or possibly the construction of a new facility. We have discovered that if people have a sense that there is a work in progress, they will not only be patient, they will partner to help you achieve your facility goals.

After the first seven minutes, when people finally enter the worship environment, make a commitment to do the best you can with what you have. Don't settle for *good enough*! Reach for ministry excellence within the context you are in. If you are not sure what to do, engage a ministry group to help you with the ministry environment. In fact, while many larger ministries are hiring full-time *ministry environment teams*, any church can engage a group of people who have some creative, cost-effective ideas. Often times, the changes or improvements that are being recommended are low-cost cosmetic enhancements that are easily sponsored by individuals within the church.

Having had the privilege of speaking in many different venues both in the United States and internationally, I can assure you that even if the building is a store front, people with a *spirit* of excellence will find a way to enhance any environment they are in. In fact, I've felt more comfortable in the worship environment of some churches that were worshipping in temporary facilities like schools, movie theaters, and store fronts than in some nice cathedrals. It can be a nice facility and still not be an environment that is conducive for worship.

My good friend Stan Toler has inspired many congregations to ministry excellence with his *Five Star Church* book, church seminars, and national conferences. He creatively communicates the principles of serving God with ministry excellence in every arena of church life. As he shares about the importance of quality in every ministry environment, he provides creative solutions that are easy for any church to incorporate. When he presented the *Five Star Church* principles to our congregation, it raised our level of awareness and commitment to ministry excellence. (I highly recommend his book for every ministry leader and worker in the local church. However, I feel even more strongly about the benefit of hosting his *Five Star Church* seminar in your local church or for a group of churches.)

CREATING A HEALTHY FINANCIAL ENVIRONMENT

Perhaps nothing negatively impacts a ministry more quickly than an unhealthy financial environment. Quite honestly, this really is one of the tightropes that we must walk down with great care and balance. On the one hand, if you don't have adequate funding, then it is impossible to fund the ministry resources or the facility enhancements that are needed. On the other hand, if you present financial needs in an unhealthy manner, it will cause people to withdraw from your existing congregation and it will deter others from wanting to become a part of your ministry.

There will be a more detailed discussion on developing a healthy growth oriented ministry budget, as well as creative funding solutions to fund your vision later in this book. But for the moment let's be clear about one absolute reality—money follows vision. Whatever you are attempting to accomplish that requires financial partnership, you must tie it to the vision of ministry. (If you don't have a clear and compelling vision – start there!)

When there is an unhealthy financial environment in a ministry, every aspect of the ministry suffers. The lack of funding impacts support for the pastor and staff, supplies for ministries, as well as the availability of space or useable space (with utilities on, insurance provided, etc.). I have been in the precarious situation of leading ministries with very limited, and, at least for a season, unhealthy levels of financial resources. The first inclination of the pastor in these cases is to simply go beyond receiving offerings for the ministry to appeals and, in some cases, either begging for money or even worse scolding people to give their money. While I believe we must present the biblical plan for the financial support for a ministry, or even a ministry project or cause, a *disproportionate* level of appeal or presentation will typically cause a reduction in financial support, not an increase.

Unfortunately, I can look back over my ministry and see specific times that I probably crossed the line into an unhealthy presentation for giving. It usually came at times of severe financial pressure and deadlines. However, while there should be and must be the ability to share the ministry budget of the church with the regular church constituents, a leader's dissatisfaction with the congregation's giving should never be shared in public.

Admittedly, in the turnaround churches I have led and the new church plant that we initiated, there have been many extremely challenging times financially. As a result, because the only training I had been exposed to was the church I grew up in, I repeated the practice that I learned from this mentoring experience. The practice was really one of *crisis giving*. Our small church had regular financial "crisis" which required desperate appeals by the leadership (typically the pastor) to the congregation. The pastors who were unwilling to make these appeals typically resigned since there was inadequate funding to support them, their families, and the ministry objectives.

For the few pastors who stayed longer than a year at my home church, their tenures were marked by various appeals based on the current crisis. This was miraculously followed by various celebrations when the pastor reported that enough money had come in to solve the current crisis. Once again, the congregation had come to the rescue. Unfortunately, this developed an unhealthy giving pattern in the church.

Most people would give *something* when the offerings were taken. If there happened to be enough money to pay the current responsibilities (and the ushers or treasurer were always to doing a quick count at the back of the sanctuary or in the church office, so they could bring a report to the pastor before the congregation was dismissed), then the members were able to keep a little extra cash in their personal budget for the week. However, if there was an inadequate amount of giving, either before the pastor preached the message or before the people were formally dismissed, there would be announcement of how much money was still needed to meet the current week's budget.

> It wasn't until a short time into my first pastorate that I realized that money follows vision.

My recollection may be distorted by my overall experience, but I would estimate that at least fifty percent of the time extra offerings had to be taken during the Sunday morning services to meet the current budget. In all of these cases, **I do not ever remember two key components being presented as it relates to giving. First, *ministry vision* was never presented, clarified, or communicated; and therefore giving was never tied to vision. Second, *stewardship education* was never a part of the spiritual formation process that was presented, other than the often repeated reminder that every person should be tithing (giving the first ten percent of their income and increase) to the work of God.** However, there was no process for stewardship education that caused the congregation to understand solid biblical teaching on financial management.

On the other hand, whenever we had a special ministry guest or missionary who powerfully presented their ministry vision, goals, and objectives, it always seemed that there was a tremendous response in giving—and the pastor would often publically announce the "wonderful and generous offering" that had been given in the service.

It wasn't until a short time into my first pastorate that I realized that money follows vision. People who support missions projects, television ministries, outreach projects, radio ministries, local ministries like rescue missions and homeless shelters, and even the local church, do so because the recipient of their generosity was able to clearly communicate their mission and vision in a clear and compelling manner. I quickly realized that if people could see the impact of their giving, they would be more generous and more consistent in their giving.

People do not want to give just to keep the utilities paid, the mortgage paid, or even the preacher paid. People give to make a difference, to touch lives, and change destinies. To the degree that I could enable the congregation to see the impact their giving was making, they would be willing to invest their financial resources in the ministry. My newfound realization caused me to repeatedly present the vision and the fruit of our efforts to the people. My goal became (and is still today) to assure people that "every time they give, somebody gets saved."

When people begin to realize that "every time they give, somebody gets saved," they'll do it with joy and gladness. However, this cannot be an empty statement. We must be able to back it up. Therefore, I've determined to find a way to assure the congregation that their giving is in fact achieving this objective, whether through our local church or through our partnership giving.

As we began to make this declaration, we began to think more intentionally about different ways people are introduced to Christ through our ministry. I believe when a church becomes intentional about its vision and ministry, it will easily produce the desired objectives that inspire people in their giving. Pastors and those who are involved in receiving offerings or who refer to giving (in cases where offerings are not formally received), should inform

> When people begin to realize that "every time they give, somebody gets saved," they'll do it with joy and gladness.

people of the impact of their giving as it relates to the mission, vision, and objectives of the church. Look for reports in the children's ministry, youth ministry, adult worship services, outreach opportunities, personal witnessing opportunities, various missionary partnerships, and other areas.

Churches are not limited to just reporting on people accepting Christ. Share reports from these different ministry groups that reflect

the fulfillment of various ministry goals and activities. Remind the congregation that through their giving the church is able to provide resources for training young children, teens and adults. Remind the congregation that through their giving they make it possible for a pastor to dedicate all or part of his time to ministry not only during the designated corporate worship times, but in the community, as well as among the homebound and institutionalized. Align the ministry with the twenty-fifth chapter of Matthew, and communicate to the congregation the different ways in which they have completed another week of feeding the hungry (at least helping one family a week with food assistance), clothing the naked (providing some new or almost-new clothing to a needy family), and visiting the sick, shut-in, and those in jail or prison.

> Total life stewardship must be an ongoing part of the spiritual formation process in the life of every believer.

At the risk of being misunderstood or making someone angry, if a ministry cannot demonstrate a legitimate ministry impact in the community and congregation on a regular basis, question whether the congregation should continue to fund the ministry. Money doesn't follow unfulfilled vision, but vision in action—a work in progress! From a biblically sound stewardship perspective, the question must be asked: "Does the ministry warrant the financial support of the congregation?" The parable of the talents might suggest that if a ministry isn't doing anything, then the resources should be given to those who are being intentional about making a difference.

A second critical piece to a healthy financial environment is a balanced and consistent stewardship education strategy. Stewardship education is a process, not just one sermon. Many pastors have discovered the value of preaching or teaching a series of stewardship messages at the beginning of each year. The stewardship series encompasses all areas of stewardship including the stewardship of time, talent (gifts and abilities), treasure (money), and their testimony (relationships). Total life stewardship must be an ongoing part of the spiritual formation process in the life of every believer. For those who have heard it before, these messages can serve as an affirmation and confirmation of the validity of their steward-ship lifestyles. (People have heard salvation messages many times, but we don't stop—or shouldn't stop—preaching them.) For those who have never heard it before, these messages are as necessary to their spiritual for-mation process as putting their faith in Christ for their salvation.

When vision is communicated in a clear and compelling manner, and balanced total life stewardship education is being provided, there will generally be sufficient resources to accomplish what the church should be doing at that time. Don't miss what I just said. There will gen-erally be sufficient resources to accomplish what the church should be doing *at that time*. Smaller congregations cannot do everything that a larger congregation may have the resources to accomplish. These smaller congregations should not feel inferior or inadequate in ministry by com-paring themselves to the opportunities that a larger congregation can pro-vide. They should focus on being faithful and fruitful with the resources they have available and be ready to do more when additional resources are available.

The vision inside of my heart today is the same vision that was inside my heart when I was serving my first congregation of thirty-five people. However, it was my responsibility to grow the people to the size of the vision, not downsize the vision to the size of the congregation. Instead of downsizing the vision, I learned to take portions of the vision that could be filled by the congregation at that time. As we grew, we could take on another portion of the vision. The vision remained the same, but the portion of the vision that we could undertake at any given time was dependent on the resources we had available to us. Even today, there are portions of the vision that God has put in my heart that we are not ready to undertake. But I'm growing the congregation to the size of the vision, not downsizing the vision to the size of the congregation.

When a pastor or ministry is able to keep its vision before the people and continue to provide total life stewardship education, it will create a healthy spiritual environment. Instead of crisis giving, people will become partners in giving to the vision on a consistent basis.

CREATING A HEALTHY SYSTEMATIC OR ORGANIZATIONAL ENVIRONMENT

Organizational health is often overlooked or ignored when considering the subject of church health and church growth. However, a ministry that is unhealthy organizationally will struggle to reach its ministry potential.

One of the best examples of the need and importance of organizational health is found in the familiar story of Moses and his journey into leadership. In the eighteenth chapter of Exodus, we discover Moses standing before long lines of people who were seeking his counsel in a wide variety of life issues. When Moses' father-in-law sees him sitting before the people all day long and the long line of people that were waiting, he speaks to him about organizational health.

Jethro informs Moses that if he continues to operate organizationally under the current system, both he and the people would wear away. His system of ministry was unhealthy and it would eventually lead to an unhealthy Moses (trying to do it all by himself) and unhealthy people (who were willing to let him do it all by himself). Jethro proceeds to give Moses an organizational system that would provide more effective ministry in a more efficient manner, thereby maximizing Moses (the man) and the people (the members).

Jethro introduces the ministry of organizational captains. In our ministry, we call this the *Captains of Ten Ministry*© or *Ministry Captains*©, because it is based on the most common assignment in the organizational structure. In this efficient and effective system introduced by Jethro, every ten people would have a ministry captain to care for them. For every group of fifty people, there would be five Captains of Ten and one Captain of Fifty. For every group of one hundred, there would be ten Captains of Ten, two Captains of Fifty, and one Captain of One Hundred. For every group of one thousand, there would be one hundred Captains of Ten, twenty Captains of Fifty, ten Captains of One Hundred, and one Captain of One Thousand. Therefore, under this efficient organizational system it would only take one hundred and thirty-one captains (caregivers/leaders) to take care of one thousand people, and every ten people would have someone specifically aware of their needs and ready to address them!

Through this organizational system, not only would these Captains of Ten become aware of the life issues of their ten people, but if a question or decision needed to be made that was too difficult for them to handle, they would simply turn to their Captain of Fifty for support. If for some reason the matter was too complex for this individual, they would turn to the Captain of One Hundred. The process would continue upward as necessary, but only allowing the most complicated matters to be presented to Moses directly.

Jethro wanted to make sure that Moses was not left feeling unneeded, so he revealed to Moses his organizational and ministry responsibilities. Moses was only to hear the most complicated matters that needed his attention or discernment, and Moses should spend his time interceding in prayer for the people (to be God-ward for the people) and to receive divine revelation from God (teaching), which he should teach to all the people (be to the people for God). Jethro concludes by saying that if you will do so, "you shall be able to endure (last) and all this people shall go to their homes in peace (needs met).

We see a similar illustration in the New Testament, in the sixth chapter of Acts, when the number of disciples was increasing rapidly and there arose a murmuring of the Grecian people against the Hebrew people because their widows were being neglected in ministry. Immediately, the apostles introduced an organizational system that would allow those who were called to pray and to proclaim the Word to remain dedicated to their focus, while a new ministry group, commonly referred to as *deacons* (servants) was selected "whom they appointed over this business."

The Apostle Paul understood the importance of systems and organization in the body of Christ. He not only compared the body of Christ to the human body, which is made up of many different systems (skeletal system, muscular system, nervous system, etc.), but he also taught the importance of ministry organization and administration in his teaching on spiritual gifts, the five-fold ministry (Ephesians 4:11-12). In addition, he appointed leadership whose responsibility it is to "set things in order" within the church by ordaining elders and deacons (Titus).

I have discovered that a ministry will either *organize* or *agonize*. The lack of organizational structure and healthy ministry systems to adequately address the day-to-day operation and ministry of the church will cause a ministry to operate ineffectively and inefficiently.

Just as there can be a lack of organizational and systematic structure that creates an unhealthy environment, there can also be excessive organizational and systematic structure that is equally damaging. On one occasion I was invited to preach at a church that only had fifteen people. When I entered the church I noticed that in this church facility every classroom doubled as an office for one of the fifteen different officers, ministers, or pastors of the church. Everyone had a title and an office, even if the office doubled as a nursery on Sunday morning. Needless to say, they had probably taken the whole idea of organization a little too far.

> Ministry will either organize or agonize.

As I have worked with many different pastors and churches, I have seen unhealthy organizational environments in which it required ten different committees to decide if the pastor could provide some emergency food assistance to a family in need within the church. Once again, we must emphasize that one of the keys to anything being *healthy* is the element of *balance*. Whether it is the proper balance of water and sunlight, as illustrated in the earlier story about the care of my wife's plants, or the amount of organization that needs to exist within a ministry in order for it to be effective and efficient, the key is *balance*.

If people within a congregation feel like there is too much bureaucratic red tape to go through in order to implement a new ministry idea or process, they will simply ignore the opportunity or seek out a place where there is less red tape. Remember, in some cases, this red tape process is simply an organizational cover for power struggles. At the same time, the absence of adequate organizational structure only produces chaos and ineffectiveness.

CREATING A HEALTHY SOCIAL
OR COMMUNITY ENVIRONMENT

Many churches fail to see the significance of having a healthy social or community environment as it relates to their church or ministry. This really has a two-fold application. First, it speaks directly to what the social conditions are in close proximity to the church. Secondly, it also refers to the importance of the community or society around the church having a healthy opinion of the ministry.

In my first place of ministry, the area around the church had become known as "Hell's forty acres." What once had been identified as a middle-class community over a period of time had undergone a significant demographic and social shift. A few weeks after I accepted this ministry opportunity, I was walking the streets of the neighborhood in my suit and tie. My name wasn't David Wilkerson, I didn't wear white leather shoes, and the place wasn't New York City, but this was going to be my "Cross and the Switchblade" story.

This was a completely new environment for me, since I was raised in a rural community with a graduating class of less than one hundred. Until my high school years the only people of color I knew were Native Americans. Although there was an element of drinking and drugs in the community where I grew up, it paled in comparison to where I now found myself.

Others before me had declared that it was time to close the church, sell the property, and relocate to a "better" neighborhood. Admittedly, there are churches that I have seen for whom this might be an adequate prescription, but only if the people who are a part of the church are unwilling to invest themselves in reaching the community around them. Inevitably, I have seen churches like this sold to other organizations or churches that consisted of people who saw the surrounding community as a great mission field of opportunity instead of an undesirable location. When the new occupants were released with a new vision, they found new ways to connect to their community and minister to them.

Even more sobering to me is the many times I had seen a Christian Church sold to an organization or religious group whose values were completely opposite of what the church represented (at least in its constitution, bylaws, or statement of faith). Within a short period of time, these organizations were flourishing because they saw the community as a gold mine, rather than a minefield. They were willing to invest in people who were for the most part hopeless and helpless and give them "another gospel." In too many instances, the Christian churches took the money and ran—and they never looked back!

I made a decision—and it is a decision that every pastor and every congregation must make. I made a decision to minister to the people within the environment that the church was located. In order for this to be effective, I had to change and our congregation had to change. The biggest area of change was our *preferences*.

On a number of occasions, some well-meaning ministers or business people that I had developed relationships with would pull me aside and ask me, "When are you going to get out of here?" Some meant, when was I going to circulate my resume for a more desirable location or church. Others meant, when was I going to sell the building and relocate the church to a more desirable location. At times, I wondered if I was actually called to the community or just being stubborn. While there were seasons and spurts of growth, there were also the challenges of a multi-ethnic congregation, made up of historical and traditional Christians, as well as former drug addicts and prostitutes.

I made a decision to minister to the people within the environment that the church was located.

During one of my times of wrestling with the volatile combination, I was impressed by the Holy Spirit to read the story of Jacob again. As I read it, I followed his story to the point in which he had worked for seven years to have Rachel as his wife only to get Leah; he then had to work another seven years to have Rachael. Shortly after this point, Jacob announces to his father-in-law that it is time for him to leave with his family and begin growing a herd of his own and to secure the posterity of his own family.

Laban quickly points out that he has been blessed since Jacob came. He began negotiating to keep him there. Jacob agreed to stay if he could start his own herd. Laban questioned how it would be possible to distinguish their herds, to which Jacob said: "Let me go through all your flocks today and remove from them every speckled or spotted sheep, every dark-colored lamb and every spotted or speckled goat. They will be my wages" (Genesis 30:32; NIV).

I read this passage several times as these words kept ringing in my ears: "I'll take the spotted ones." Jacob had made a decision that he would take the portion of the flock that was considered by human perspective as inferior or less valuable.

> As I accepted the challenge of letting God change me—before he changed the people he had sent me to—God did exactly what he promised.

He did not argue over the pure-breeds or the unblemished ones; he simply chose the spotted ones, which were considered less healthy or fruitful in reproduction. However, reading on in the story, God gave Jacob a plan that caused his herd to reproduce faster than the pure-breeds. Then I felt the Holy Spirit impress upon me, "That's why I want to do for you—take the spotted ones."

With a fiery passion of enthusiasm, I shared the vision with the congregation through a series of messages entitled: "I'll take the spotted ones." I thought everyone would be as enthusiastic as I was about my revelation, but I quickly learned that even people who came from horrific backgrounds didn't really like the idea of being called "spotted ones." Eventually, I was able to help them understand that in reality we are all "the spotted ones." We all have been spotted by sin. There is "none righteous, no not one." "We have all sinned and come short of the glory of God." Some of our spots may seem bigger or more visible than others. The reality is that some people have spots on their skin (visible areas of their life), while others have spots on their internal organs (the hidden areas of their life).

As I accepted the challenge of letting God change me—before he changed the people he had sent me to—God did exactly what he promised. In just three short years, the ministry flourished to over four hundred in attendance. God had made us more fruitful than many other ministries who had focused on people with smaller (or perhaps cosmetically covered up) spots.

I'm not suggesting that only ministries that focus on drug addicts, prostitutes, or other socially challenged people can grow or are doing God's will. I have seen successful business people, even millionaires, that spiritually speaking were "the spotted ones." **What I am suggesting is that every ministry needs to decide whether or not it will accept the challenge, whether it has the desire and the ministry gifts necessary to reach the community and society around its present location.** If our community had significantly shifted to Spanish-speaking people, it would have been better for us to make our facility available to a Christian Spanish-speaking ministry, either through a shared facility or by selling or donating the facility to them. However, if a congregation has the vision, burden, passion, and gift mix to reach the people surrounding the proximity of the church, they should engage and embrace the community. If they don't have the vision, burden, passion, or gift mix, they should allow those who do to have access to the facility under some arrangement.

As the church engages and embraces its community, it will discover creative ways to minister to the needs, concerns, and interest of the people and create *ministry bridges* that will allow the congregation to reach them and will allow the community to cross over to the ministries of the church.

In the second application, it is important for the church to have a good reputation in the community in which it is located. I'm concerned about ministries that are known on the other side of the world for their missions projects, but the people two blocks away don't even know the church exists. I'm concerned about ministries that are known by their denomination or ministry affiliations as a great church because of all of their programming and giving, but they have never built a ministry bridge to the people within their own community and sphere of geographical influence.

At the same time, I'm concerned about churches that are very well known in their community, but what they are known for is not good. One church that I served was very well known in the community by virtue of its physical presence and geographical location, sitting at the crossroads of two major freeways. However, the reputation of the church in the years just prior to my arrival had been tainted by several undesirable experiences. In addition to two pastors leaving in a short period of time, with both marriages ending in divorce shortly thereafter, and the closing of the Christian school just a couple of weeks before classes were to begin, there was another cloud hanging over the ministry.

A few years earlier, a well-known evangelist had conducted a series of services in this church. During his visit, he prayed for a woman who had come to the altar for prayer. As he prayed for her she fell to the ground, in what the evangelist interpreted to simply be the overwhelming presence of God. It was later determined that when she fell to the ground that there was a complication from the fall which eventually resulted in her death.

When I began introducing myself to people in the community, I would ask them if they knew the church, and if so, what did they know? Many people knew about the two pastoral transitions and divorces or the closing of the school, which had been covered in the local news. Other times people would say, "That's the church where the evangelist killed the woman." Needless to say, getting people to respond to invitations to the altar was very difficult in my first few years at the church.

It was clear to me that the church had a well-defined presence in the community, but it wasn't the one we wanted. Once again, I began to pray for direction about how to overcome this unhealthy social environment. Through this process, I was brought to the experience surrounding the death of John the Baptist. I imagined what it must have been like for Jesus and His disciples as they were trying to launch the ministry of Jesus to the world, only to hear the report that the forerunner of Jesus had been killed. (This could definitely put a damper on new member recruitment and people wanting to participate in your vision!)

As I read through the story many times (especially in the fourteenth chapter of Matthew), I noticed that when Jesus heard that John the Baptist had been killed, he left by ship into a desert place (Matthew 14:13). Undoubtedly, this gave him the time and opportunity to deal with his personal sorrow regarding the loss of John the Baptist, but perhaps also to initiate a plan to get beyond this "negative publicity."

When Jesus gets off the ship, he is met by a great multitude of people. He immediately begins ministering to them until the day has gone long. The disciples recommend sending the people away to their homes to get something to eat and a night's rest, so they could return the next day. Jesus, however, responds in a manner that catches his disciples off guard, by suggesting they should feed the multitude. The story unfolds quickly as Jesus takes a little boy's lunch of five loaves of bread and two small fish, blesses them, and then distributes them to his disciples, who in turn will distribute it to about five thousand men (plus women and children). (Don't miss the importance of a healthy organizational system. Luke's Gospel indicates that he made them sit down in groups of fifties.)

The interesting point here is that this is the only miracle of Jesus (outside of his death, burial, and resurrection) that is recorded in all four of the Gospels. No other miracle performed by Jesus on behalf of a specific person or group of people is recorded in all four Gospels. This indicated to me that there was something very intentional about Jesus feeding the five thousand men, plus their families. From that moment on, people are no longer talking about the death of John the Baptist, they are talking about the feeding of five thousand.

When I realized the significance, I immediately said, "We need a *feeding-five-thousand* experience to cause people to forget the past and to position or reposition the church's influence in the community in a positive light." I began sharing a series of messages with the congregation that focused on impacting the lives of five thousand people each month in as many different ways as we could. This brought about the introduction of our "*Impact 5000©*" or "*I5K©*" ministries. Our attendance at the time we began this initiative was around five hundred people. Obviously, this would be a challenge for us to minister to a group of people ten times larger than our present congregation.

As I began to share the messages with the congregation, their heart and spirit began to open to the possibilities, and then we began. The first month, the goal was to collect five thousand cans of soup, which we would give to the various rescue missions, shelters, and food banks in our city. The second month we collected five thousand pairs of socks to give to children in schools who did not have adequate covering for the feet in the cold months. Each month we did something to impact the lives of five thousand people.

Finally, there came the day that I announced to the congregation that I wanted our church to invite five thousand people onto our campus, so we could give them a free meal, give their school-age children free backpacks and school supplies as they prepared to return to school, and to give them a presentation of the Gospel. My experience was in many ways, just like the one Jesus had. Immediately people begin to say, "Do you know how much that will cost?" We had our own financial "Miracle of the Feeding of 5000!"

Although we didn't actually experience the miracle of a small amount of food being supernaturally multiplied as we distributed it to the people, what we did experience was a new identity in the community. No longer were we the church where two pastor's marriages fell apart, where a school closed just days before the school year was to begin, or where an evangelist killed a woman. From that point on, we were known as the church that was feeding five thousand people and giving school supplies to children.

I do not want to suggest that the church was or is perfect, or even that it has fully reached its potential. But I do want to suggest that the church was and is on its way to fulfilling its God-given destiny, because they worked to position the church within a healthy social or community environment. Every church must be a work in progress. We are not what we will be, but we certainly are not what we were. We are a work in progress. We were, in fact, connecting the dots within our ministry environments.

CHAPTER FIVE

MORE "MINISTRY DOTS" TO CONNECT!

In addition to the internal and external positioning that must take place in relationship to the seven healthy environments, I have identified *ten critical areas of ministry life and organization that also requir positioning*. My personal experience as a pastor and consultant has caused me to identify ten areas that exist within every church ministry that must be properly connected in order for the vision to be realized. Our experience has been that to the degree that the church can effectively position the ministry properly in each of these ten areas, the church will not only be healthy, but it will be growing.

More time is spent exploring each of these ten areas in our *Positioning Your Church* connecting-the-dots seminars and conferences, which enable a church both to assess the health of the church in each area and to identify potential solutions for each one. In addition, there is incredible value in requesting one of our consultants for a *Positioning Your Church* ministry assessment for an individual church, along with a one-year coaching relationship, to help connect the dots and assist in navigating the implementation of the strategic Ministry Action Plan. Additional resources also exist to assist churches in conducting a self-assessment in each of these areas and to apply potential prescriptive solutions. However, for the scope of this book, we will simply identify and briefly describe each of the ten areas which we have found to be critical in the overall health and mobilization of a local church.

1. POSITIONING THE VISION OF THE CHURCH

The first area of church life and organization that must be positioned is the vision of the church. Keeping in mind (or reviewing, if necessary) the definition of positioning, the vision of the church involves the communication of a desired future that requires the cooperation and coordination of the pastor(s), leadership, congregation, resources, facilities, ministry schedule, and community.

The prophet Habakkuk recorded the instructions of the Lord as it relates to positioning the vision of the church and all of these various components and entities that are associated with the vision.

> Then the LORD answered me and said: "Write the vision and make it plain on tablets, That he may run who reads it. For the vision is yet for an appointed time; but at the end it will speak, and it will not lie. Though it tarries, wait for it; because it will surely come, It will not tarry."
>
> Habakkuk 2:2-3 (NKJV)

From this familiar passage of scripture we realize that God is the source of the vision, which he revealed to a prophet or leader and was to be written down and made plain (clear and compelling), that people who read it would run with the vision. We can also see there are scheduling and timing issues, which further confirm the elements of coordination and cooperation.

God is the source of the vision.

When an assessment of a vision or vision statement occurs, there are specific elements that must be present. Among these elements, there must also be a foundational mission statement which refocuses the church on their primary reason for being. As stated earlier, many churches that are in decline or are plateaued are suffering from *mission drift*. The absence of a simple and concise mission statement will cause the vision of the church to be foundationless.

The process of positioning the vision of the church must start with knowing your mission and reigniting the passion of the people for this core value and purpose. It is my firm conviction that a mission statement should be clearly and simply stated in a brief sentence that is easy to remember and easily recited by the congregation. However, additional explanation and support information should be available to further define key components of the mission statement.

Once there is absolute clarity as to the mission of the church, the next step is to define, clarify, and quantify your mission into your vision statement. In other words, a vision statement should take your mission and clarify it within the context of the local church and community and quantify it into a measurable and focused direction. Vision must be more than a number; it must be what will happen in the lives of those who are identified as the focus of your ministry, when the vision is fulfilled.

Although vision must be more than a number, I believe it is important to incorporate numerical values as a part of the assessment of vision process. Numbers should be used to measure health and stewardship of people, resources, and ministries. If a church wants to establish a numerical goal for its vision, it is best to establish this goal based on health goals and on the stewardship of existing or future resources.

For example, if a church determined that the maximum number of people they could serve from their current facility is one thousand people (using multiple services and having access to a sufficient population to draw from), then a ministry might want to establish a numerical stewardship goal of reaching and serving one thousand people. Any numerical goals that are established must be challenging, yet achievable; therefore maximum stewardship numerical goals are typically phased over a period of time.

If a church wants to reach a larger number of people or increase the stewardship goal for its ministry, there must be a strategic solution for securing the resources needed to accomplish the higher goal. We call this strategic solution a Strategic M.A.P. (Ministry Action Plan). In this process, a church's vision is developed into a strategic ministry action plan that includes both stewardship goals (based on what is available at the present time) and strategic goals (based on what will become available through strategic planning and growth).

Positioning the vision of the church involves developing a strategic ministry action plan to fulfill the vision. The Strategic M.A.P. must be an intentional plan, which is not vague or immeasurable. It must incorporate strategic objectives for implementation over a sufficient period of time—coordinating people, resources, and opportunities for maximum effectiveness.

In our *Positioning Your Church* training events and resources, we identify seven factors that are critical in defining, clarifying, and quantifying your mission statement into your vision statement, which is then incorporated into your strategic ministry action plan. By understanding and developing an intentional response to each of the seven factors, you can then create a customized, clear, and compelling vision.

Positioning the vision of the church goes beyond the development of a mission statement, vision statement, and strategic ministry action plan; it also incorporates vision-casting. Vision-casting is the communication of a vision in such a manner that it captures the heart, imagination, and emotions of people, inspiring and inviting them to invest their time, energy, and resources in the fulfillment of the vision.

Effective vision-casting requires communicating a compelling vision which leaves a mental or visual imprint on the mind and heart of those who hear and see it. Vision-casting involves painting a clear picture of the future with compelling words, stories, illustrations, and an unlimited variety of visuals to enhance the communication process.

A compelling vision which leaves a mental or visual imprint on the mind and heart of those who hear and see it.

The result of a clear and compelling vision that has been effectively communicated will be the ability to secure the necessary resources and partnerships to fulfill the vision. This not only involves "counting the cost" of your vision, but also the objective of developing strategic partnerships with people and organizations that are critical to the success and fulfillment of the vision.

Many visions fail to be fulfilled because of inadequate resources and partnerships. A lack of resources is not an indication that the vision should not be fulfilled; it is an indication of an insufficient amount of time having been spent or allocated on effective vision development, vision casting, and relational development. Relational development within both the church and the community must be genuine and passionate. The relationship should not be built on how a church can benefit from the person or organization, but what value can the church add to their life or organization.

When people are confident that a church genuinely and passionately cares about their cause and about helping others to find significance, meaning, and fulfillment in their life or organization, they will offer their partnership and resources to see the vision fulfilled. Building strategic partnerships not only includes building strong donor relationships, but also strategic partnerships with ministries and organizations that can assist the church in fulfilling its vision.

Earlier I made an emphatic statement that "money follows vision." Before vision attracts financial support, it must first capture the heart of the donor. Before people will give their financial support you must win their emotional and spiritual support. Effective vision development and vision-casting accomplishes this objective, allowing the words of the Lord to prophet Habakkuk to be realized in every ministry. "For the vision is yet for an appointed time; but at the end it will speak, and it will not lie. Though it tarries, wait for it; because it will surely come, It will not tarry." (Habakkuk 2:3, NKJV)

> Before people will give their financial support you must win their emotional and spiritual support.

2. POSITIONING THE PASTOR OF THE CHURCH

Once a clear and compelling vision has been defined, the next most significant factor in church health and growth is the pastor. *It has been clearly documented in our work with thousands of pastors and churches around the world that the most important human factor in church health and church growth is the pastor.* While we will quickly point out that there are other significant human factors such as church leadership, volunteers, congregation, and community, the pastor will play the most significant and strategic role in the area of church health and church growth.

First and foremost, the pastor should always be developing or growing in three critical areas.

SPIRITUAL FORMATION

While this may be downplayed, over-looked, or even ignored by many, the spiritual development of the pastor is a critical component in church health and church growth. If a pastor is not growing spiritually, it will result in spiritual stagnation or decline of the congregation, which will ultimately manifest in the overall health, attendance, and effectiveness of the church. If pastors are not growing spiritually, they cannot and will not be sharing fresh and challenging insights through the preaching and teaching of the Word of God.

SKILL FORMATION

Many pastors have at least attended a few seminars or read a few books on leadership and possibly a few other subjects related to their role as a pastor or ministry leader. However, by and large, the skill set which most pastors developed before they entered into the ministry and within the first five years of ministry, is the same skill set they are using today. It is estimated that only five to ten percent of all pastors, staff members, and leaders in ministry today have a plan or are intentionally developing their ministry skills. There is a direct correlation between this five to ten percent of leaders and the five to ten percent of all churches that are growing. Growing churches have growing pastors, especially in the area of skill formation.

STRATEGIC FORMATION

Unfortunately, a tremendous number of pastors, staff members, and church leaders have come to believe that if they pray, read their Bible, and possibly develop in a few key areas of leadership, this will be sufficient to lead a ministry in health and growth. Most pastors have not been exposed to the necessity and value of strategic planning and implementation, and therefore very few have actually developed in this area. Strategic formation involves developing the ability to connect the dots of ministry through proper diagnosis, identifying potential prescriptive solutions, and implementing a strategic ministry action plan. In our additional *Positioning Your Church* resources, training, and assessments, we cultivate the ability of the pastor and leader to provide the on-going assessment and prescriptive solutions for their ministry.

A second critical area of positioning as it relates to the pastor is the development of the pastor's ability to understand and embrace leadership transitions through the various stages of church health and church growth. Many pastors have a basic understanding of the reality that the manner in which a minister would lead a church of thirty-five is different than the way they would lead three hundred or three thousand. As the church goes through various transitions of size and health, the pastor must understand the role they should fulfill during each of these stages. This means not only being equipped to do so, but also remaining flexible, mentally and spiritually.

Growing churches require a pastor to become more efficient and effective in vision-casting and administration, while also increasing in the quality of their pulpit ministry. Pastors of declining or plateaued churches typically spend two to four hours per sermon in prayer and preparation, while pastors of growing churches typically spend between eight and twelve hours per sermon in prayer and preparation. The ability of pastors of growing churches to do so is the result of their team-building skills. The inability of pastors of declining or plateaued churches is typically the result of not having built sufficient ministry teams, meaning they must personally do more of the ministry maintenance and care, leaving less time for prayer and preparation.

Pastors of growing churches discover one of the most effective and efficient things they can do in their ministry is to engage in the process of ministry, member, and leader multiplication through coaching and team-building. While many pastors may like to view themselves as a coach or team-builder, it is only a reality when they are no longer evaluated and appreciated by what they do themselves, but what they can get done through others (teams). We have discovered that a church or ministry will most likely never grow beyond one hundred and fifty people until the leader transitions from shepherding individuals and begins equipping others for ministry through team-building.

Without team-building, the size of a leader's vision (or a church's vision) is limited to how much time and energy the leader (pastor) can personally commit to the cause. When ministry teams are built, the vision of the pastor and leader becomes unlimited or only limited by the number of ministry teams the pastor or church develops.

The fact remains that people are more motivated, more personally fulfilled, and gain greater ownership in ministry when they are a part of a ministry team. The individuals who are to be served by the ministry benefit more from the expansion, efficiency, and effectiveness of ministry that is provided through ministry teams than through the more limited ministry of an individual pastor or staff member serving alone.

3. POSITIONING THE LEADERS OF THE CHURCH

Positioning the leaders in the church involves clarifying the significant roles of different church leaders (staff, board, ministry and department leaders, etc.) and knowing how to position and empower them in facilitating the mission and vision of the church, which is essential to church health and church growth. This requires the pastors to grow in their leadership capacity to not only be a leader of people, but to be a leader of leaders. If pastors are not viewed as leaders of leaders, it will be difficult, if not impossible for them to position the leadership of the church for health and growth.

It is important to identify and understand the perspective of each church leader. When I first came to one of the churches I led, I asked each of the leaders to identify their involvement and role in the church as they viewed it. As we went around the room hearing each person share their perspective, I was stunned to hear one individual specifically say: "My job is to protect the church from the pastor!" I was shocked, but he was serious. This board member viewed his divine assignment as one of protectionism— specifically protecting the church from me as the newly elected pastor.

Obviously, this perspective was unhealthy for any board member to have, but the fact that no one corrected the statement let me know that there was a need for repositioning the leadership mindset of the church. Somewhere along the line, the conduct of the previous pastor or pastors had left a bad taste in this board member's mouth. At a minimum, the conduct of the past had raised serious questions in the minds of the remaining board members and caused their perspective to be unhealthy at best.

Through a few bad experiences, coupled with the transitional gaps between pastors that shifted many of the day-to-day decision-making responsibilities to these board members, the leadership had adopted a *permission-giving* perspective on their assignment. As I presented my recommendations for the future, there was clearly an understanding that everything needed to pass by them for approval. While I certainly understand accountability, especially in the area of finances, I do not believe that having a leadership team that views its role as *giving permission* to the ideas and recommendations of the pastor is the best arrangement.

It has been my experience personally, as well as in the various ministries that I have been associated with as a coach or consultant, that the healthiest pastor-board relationships occur when the pastor is allowed to cast the vision and the board views their role as *vision-supportive* rather than *permission-giving*. Instead of voting on whether or not to fund or approve the recommendations presented by the pastor in a permission-giving environment, healthy church boards view their role as finding a way to fund and facilitate the vision and recommendations of the pastor. While the shift in perspective and process may seem subtle, they are significant.

A second area of positioning with the church's leadership involves paid staff members and ministry leaders. Perhaps inherent with the fact that a vast percentage of congregations have less than one hundred people and are led by a solo pastor, this pattern evolves into the ministries of churches that have multiple staff or even volunteer or part-time ministry leaders. The pattern is that of the solo leader who is a *doer* of ministry, rather than a *facilitator* and *equipper* of ministry.

The biggest growth challenge in pastors and their staff members is the stage that requires them to equip and empower other leaders for ministry—and then let them lead it. I have seen staff members who recruited a large number of team members, only to have the team watch the staff member do all of the ministry. In my opinion, with only a very few exceptions, the typical staff member should not be hired to do a ministry, but to develop ministry teams to do the ministry.

I would rather have a children's pastor who can train, equip, empower, and release six teams of children's ministry workers who provide ministry to children and their families, than to have one children's pastor who had the ability to hold the attention of five hundred children. Likewise, I would rather have a youth pastor who can build student ministry teams and adult sponsor teams and provide them with the support and encouragement they need to be effective and successful, than to have a youth pastor who has the ability to rally five hundred youth. I would also rather have an adult ministry pastor who can build multiple ministry teams for small groups, adult education classes, specialized ministries, and even member care, than to have one adult ministry pastor who is exhausted from trying to do it all alone.

> People are more motivated, more personally fulfilled, and gain greater ownership in ministry when they are a part of a ministry team.

I constantly stress to the staff members on my teams that I do not want them to do ministry alone. Staff members should always have a team with them, a team they have empowered to do a task or that they are mentoring for ministry. I want them to report how many new people have become involved in ministry service under their leadership, not just how many people benefited from their ministry activities for another week.

In addition to having leadership with a lack of proper training or healthy perspective, there may also be a crisis of qualified and available leadership. There is a need to identify and develop new leaders within any ministry that desires to grow. **The leadership base of the church must be constantly expanding to accommodate the growth and expansion that is a part of the vision of the church.** This requires a commitment from both the pastor (and where applicable) the staff to be constantly:

- Identifying potential leaders.
- Inviting potential leaders to become a part of a training and leadership development process.
- Influencing existing and potential leaders through vision-casting, training, and education.
- Investing in existing and potential leaders with your time, resources, conferences, seminars, retreats, and appreciation.
- Involving existing and potential leaders in dreaming, planning, implementation, and celebration.
- Inspiring existing and potential leaders to use their personal and ministry influence for the benefit of the ministry and others.
- Introducing existing and potential leaders to ministry covenant and commitment.
- Explaining how they can extend or restart the life cycle of the ministry through their incorporation of new leaders, new influencers, and new ideas.

4. POSITIONING THE VOLUNTEERS OF THE CHURCH

One of the discoveries that I made very early in ministry was the fact that, in many ways, a pastor or a church is only as good as its volunteers. Collectively and individually, volunteers directly impact and influence the people with whom they come into contact. *Many times, energy and resources that had been invested to attract people to experience the ministry opportunities is completely wasted and undermined in less than thirty seconds by a volunteer's encounter with a member or guest.* However, on the other hand, I can also assure you that there are many occasions in which ministry volunteers cause the ministry to be more effective and more desirable to people because of their outstanding service.

Much like the owner of any business, who cannot be at the front door greeting every customer or serving those who are interested in the goods and services offered by the business, pastors cannot do it all alone. On more than one occasion, I excused myself from a restaurant or business shaking my head, wondering what the owner of this business would do if they knew what I had just experienced. Every good business person knows that if they do it all themselves for the purposes of maintaining quality and control, they will limit the size of their business. But if they can engage in employee training programs for customer service and quality control, they can expand their influence and impact.

> A local church's ministries will never be better than their volunteers.

Pastors and leaders of the church and its various ministries must understand these same principles. A local church's ministries will never be better than their volunteers. However, very few churches invest time, energy, or resources in volunteer training for ministry service or quality control. As a result, there can be a great music ministry and great pulpit ministry in a church, but because the support ministries to the children, youth, and families are unhealthy, the actions of these volunteers often undermine the influence and impact of the church.

I often share a story about a time when I was vision-casting my passion for reaching as many young families and their children as possible. In my excitement, I announced in the message that I wanted us to add fifty new babies in the nursery by the end of the year. I was excited and most of the congregation was, but the workers in the nursery didn't share my passion or my excitement. The thought of increasing their ministry load by fifty new babies, when they already felt outnumbered ten to one, left them somewhat less than enthusiastic, to say the least.

I imagined what it might be like for a new young couple visiting the church. Prior to coming to the sanctuary, they would make their way to the nursery to place their children in the early childhood ministry. Can you imagine what they would have done if they had been met by a nursery volunteer who looked exhausted, distraught, and frazzled at the check in counter? Can you imagine how they might have responded if the volunteer began to explain the overload in the nursery and the significantly higher number of babies and toddlers than workers? Can you imagine what the guests might have done if the volunteer proceeded to ask them to sign a waiver of liability before placing their children in the nursery, which provided protection from legal liability in the event their child had any bruises or broken bones, or if they failed to feed or change the child while in their care? This young family would not have signed the waiver; they would have taken their children and left—not just the nursery, they would have left the church.

Although I have no knowledge of such an experience ever happening within our ministry, I can tell you that when a young family arrives at the infant check-in center, and they are met by a volunteer or representative who looks at the family and their children, rolls their eyes, or gives a long exhausted sigh, the volunteer communicates everything in the previous paragraph, condensed down to a sigh. The young families will leave, never come back, and even worse—they will tell all of the young families they know about their experience.

With this in mind, we must make significant investments in our ministry volunteers. In doing so, we must emphasize seven types of ministry, each of which are explored in an in-depth manner in our conferences, seminars and assessments.

- **Vision-based ministry**. Let them see the big picture and the significant contribution they are making to the entire process.
- **Prayer-based ministry**. We must not only pray for people to become involved in ministry, we must pray for the people who are involved in ministry.
- **Relationship-based ministry**. Healthy personal relationships

among volunteers will provide personal, emotional, physical, and spiritual renewal.

- **Gift-based ministry**. Every person has at least one spiritual or ministry gift that God wants them to use to fulfill their purpose in life, so they may experience a sense of fulfillment and significance. We need to help them identify and develop these gifts and provide them a place of service.

- **Faith-based ministry**. Some new ministries will need to be started based on faith, believing that God is inspiring the congregation to enter into a new area of ministry and that the personnel and resources will become available after a period of sacrifice.

- **Strategic or Systems-based ministry**. Just as God created the human body with different systems (nerves, muscles, circulation, etc.) and structures (skeleton), the Body of Christ was intended to function through systems and structures. The ministry systems of the church should be healthy, effective, and relevant, while having sufficient resources to fulfill their objectives; otherwise ministry partners will quickly become frustrated and quit.

- **Team-based ministry**. Throughout the Bible we see God's plan for team-based ministry. God used all different sizes of teams, whether they were the smaller teams of two, seven, or twelve; or medium-size teams of seventy or one hundred and twenty; or even larger teams of three hundred (Gideon), four hundred (David), Moses' captains of tens, fifties, hundreds, and thousands, or many others.

5. POSITIONING THE CONGREGATION

In order to position the congregation for growth, it is typically necessary for the pastor to understand the role of leading from the pulpit. This process incorporates more than simply sharing a message of what should be done, but also influencing people to demonstrate the right attitude and action in every situation. **One particular area of positioning the congregation will be in their acceptance and accommodating new people as they express an interest in the church and ministry through their participation.**

I remember one Sunday in which it became clear to me that I had not adequately positioned the church for the new people that we were developing relationships with. On this particular Sunday morning there was a new family sitting in a specific location that is typically occupied by a long-standing member of the church. The person I am referring to always arrived late and made a grand entrance shuffling across the front of the church like Tim Conway when he played Mr. Whiggins in the Carol Burnett show. Of course, he waited to make his grand entrance during the worship service, waiving his hand at the crowd like it was a Thanksgiving Day Parade, while supporting himself with a walking cane in the other hand. When he reached the row from which he always enjoyed the service, the guest family was there. He proceeded to hit the man on the leg, insisting that they needed to move out of his location.

While not all churches have people that will beat their guests out of certain seating sections, the same thing occurs when people enter the sanctuary or classroom early so they can strategically place their coats, Bibles, or other "markers" on certain seats to reserve their spot. When the guest arrives, they simply see a sign that says, "No Trespassing." We cover several areas in our training and assessments that must be addressed with the congregation in order to respond properly to growth and new people.

In addition to the receptivity of the congregation to new people and new growth, it is necessary to position the church for health and growth by addressing the congregation's spiritual and emotional morale. It may be necessary to address the congregation's comfort or change quotient. How willing is the congregation to embrace change for the purpose of reaching new people?

In every case we have been involved in, it was necessary for the pastor to spend sufficient time positioning the church's response to the mission and vision of the church. A congregation's *commitment* is a decision on their part to invest their available time, energy, and resources to see the mission and vision of the church fulfilled. A congregation's *passion* determines the degree to which people will invest themselves. A congregation's *sacrifice* occurs when a person is willing to go above and beyond the call of duty to give sacrificially.

All of these areas and many others are elements that exist within the congregation, which the pastor and leaders must properly address by developing a strategic ministry action plan.

6. POSITIONING THE COMMUNITY

In the earlier section regarding positioning the church in a healthy community environment, I pointed out the importance of cultivating and developing a healthy community relationship in which to do ministry. I also pointed out that every church needs to identify specific ministries they feel equipped to provide, which can be used as *bridge ministries* to connect the church to the community and the community to the church.

This reference to positioning the community more directly involves creating a community awareness of the church or ministry through a variety of methods. This may be accomplished through at least three types of ministries:

Incorporate a Community Awareness Campaign

First, a church should determine what the community's opinion is, if any, regarding the local church, and then develop a plan to replace any absence of awareness with a positive awareness and any negative opinions with positive experiences. By incorporating a community awareness campaign, the church can get its message out and its presence known through many different strategies including, but not limited to:

- Word-of-mouth excitement and invite cards
- Community impact ministries and projects
- Church hosted website and church utilized websites
- Printed media (flyers, signs, banners, billboards)
- Electronic Media (internet, TV, radio, etc.)

- Appreciation events for community agencies and individuals
- Providing free services (weddings, funerals, baby dedications, counseling, etc.)

Intentional Evangelism Strategy

I have discovered that approximately ninety-five percent of the evangelical churches in America do not have an intentional evangelism strategy. Once again, this may also correlate to the fact that only five percent of all churches in America are growing through conversions (and not transfer of believers or members). Within these growing ministries there are a variety of intentional evangelism strategies, such as:

- Personal friendship evangelism strategies.
- Marketplace evangelism
- Special interest evangelism (i.e., sports)
- Compassion evangelism (food, clothing, medical, etc.)
- Special event evangelism (crusades, concerts, holiday presentations, etc.)
- Evangelistic dramas or productions
- Internet evangelism
- Media evangelism (TV, radio)
- Child evangelism activities (backyard Bible clubs, kid's crusades, VBS)
- Youth evangelism activities
- Family evangelism activities
- Single adult evangelism activities
- Senior adult evangelism activities
- Special needs evangelism activities

Every church can find an intentional group of people to reach or intentional ministries to implement. Regardless of what a church does, it should be intentional!

Community Service Strategy

Churches that implement community service strategies understand the importance of bridge ministries and third place ministries. These are ministries that offer a neutral site or neutral environment in which a specific service is provided for the benefit of the participant, with the only other goal of the church being relationship development. These ministries focus on *showing* Jesus, not just *sharing* Jesus.

- Children's day care or mother's day out
- Senior adult daytime activity center
- Second language classes (Spanish, English, etc.)
- Pre-marital counseling classes
- Parenting classes
- Marriage and family enrichment classes and family counseling services
- Free family-life seminars (How to Drug-Proof Your Kids, How to Affair Proof Your Marriage, etc.)
- Free health services (blood pressure, blood drive, chiropractic, etc.)
- Educational services (tutoring, mentoring, adult continuing education, etc.)
- Job training opportunities
- Training to develop better job interview skills
- Hosting job fairs (inviting businesses to set up displays and interview booths)
- How to start your own business classes or seminars (learn from experienced entrepreneurs)
- Free financial planning and money management workshops
- Time or life management classes
- Exercise or weight loss classes
- Support groups (Grief Care, Divorce Care, Divorce Care for Kids, substance abuse, etc.)
- Music classes (community vocal groups, instrument training)
- Drama classes (community plays and productions)
- CRP and safety training
- Disaster relief and emergency response teams

The opportunities for impacting and influencing a community are unlimited. As the church begins to think intentionally about the opportunities within the community and the gifts, talents, and abilities within the congregation, the church will begin positioning itself in the community.

7. POSITIONING THE CHURCH FACILITY

I identified the church facility as one of the seven health environments that is critical to the church's effectiveness in ministry. The application and focus in this area not only includes the first impressions and general condition, but also the stewardship and strategic use of your church facility. Positioning your facility not only includes the elements of access, location, first impressions, curb appeal, exterior and interior signage, smell, and cleanliness, but we must also evaluate the best use of space.

In each place that I have had the privilege of serving as the pastor, one of the first things I did was to determine the stewardship appearance and stewardship capacity of the facility I had to work with. **First, are we doing all we can to provide the best environment (appearance and atmosphere) for worship and support ministries as possible?** People with a spirit of excellence can and will take any environment, whether it is a one hundred year old building, storefront, public school, or a newly constructed facility, and they will apply the spirit of excellence in every area.

Secondly, pastors and leaders must obtain an honest stewardship assessment of what is the realistic stewardship capacity of the facility we have access to. Unless the church is in a rented environment in which there is limited time access, all other ministries could at least double their stewardship capacity by adding a second time for ministry; and they could triple their stewardship capacity by adding a third time for ministry. The more times that ministry opportunities can be offered within a church facility, the better stewardship of facility is taking place.

Thirdly, churches must evaluate what their strategic capacity is by not limiting their evaluation for maximum use to the time commitment

required for a pastor, staff, ministry leaders, and volunteers to lead multiple services. Instead, these churches should consider the possibility of allowing their facility to be used at other times by other Christian churches, such as new churches, displaced churches, and different language churches.

Fourthly, it may be necessary for the pastor and leaders to position the church for enhancements and expansion of an existing church facility, or possibly selling an existing property, and the implementation of a relocation strategy. I am convinced that, in many cases, the reason for a church's inability to grow is not its location (there are a few exceptions). However, I am persuaded that when a congregation no longer has a desire or interest to worship in its current facility or environment, or does not feel they have the gifts, talents, and ability to reach the people surrounding the current facility, then it may be in the best interest of the group to relocate their ministry. However, if the church relocates, it must do so in a demographic location in which they are willing and able to invest themselves in reaching out to the community.

8. POSITIONING THE CHURCH FINANCES

Most churches have allocated all of their funding to feeding the flock and maintaining or providing a facility, leaving no financial resources to reach unbelievers or to expand their ministry teams. However, adequate funding is necessary for church health. The church budget must provide adequate funding for staff, facilities, and resources to effectively minister directly to those who are currently being served by ministry, as well as to reach those whom they desire to serve in ministry.

I have discovered that most churches are budgeted for maintenance or decline and not for growth. This is reflected in the allocations that are made for staff, facilities, ministry resources, as well as outreach, evangelism, and missions. In our assessments, we have discovered the value of a percentage-based budget in the allocation of funding. In our work with churches, we have discovered the following percentages or allocations were consistently found in growing churches. All other churches had a disproportionate skew of financial allocations which significantly impacted the ability of the church or ministry to grow.

In our assessments, we have discovered that growing churches with growing budgets typically divided their budget into four areas with the following percent allocation.

- **Staffing.** Typically forty to fifty percent of the tithes and undesignated offerings are budgeted for personnel. This is most significantly skewed in smaller churches where a pastor may receive a higher percentage of the tithes. However, we have repeatedly recorded evidence that when more than fifty percent of a church's budget is spent on staffing costs, other areas of the budget are inadequately funded, which impairs the growth potential of the church.
- **Facility.** Typically twenty-five to thirty-five percent of the tithes and undesignated offerings are spent on the church campus. This number may be significantly lower if a ministry has a debt free facility. However, even in these cases, we recommend that at least twenty-five percent of the budget be set aside for facility operations (utilities, insurance, etc.), maintenance and repairs, and future enhancements and expansion projects. This percentage will often increase to thirty-five percent of the church's budget when there is debt service for a new facility. The additional ten percent must either come from other areas of the budget or there must be a capital stewardship campaign in place to bear the additional facility expenses.
- **Ministry Resources.** Typically fifteen to twenty percent of the tithes and undesignated offerings are assigned to ministry resources. These resources may include curriculum and ministry tools for children, youth, and adults. These resources also include office equipment and supplies, mailing costs, and printing costs. Any items that are needed for ministry support would be included within this portion of the budget, such as musical equipment and ministry transportation vehicles.
- **Evangelism, Outreach, and Missions.** Typically ten to fifteen percent of the tithes and undesignated offerings are assigned to this

category. Some organizations require a cooperative giving plan to which most if not all of this portion of the budget is assigned. However, when possible, a church should use this percentage to underwrite the various outreach and evangelism projects developed by the strategic action team of the local church and generate the additional denominational support through designated giving or fundraising projects. Regardless of where the funding comes from, churches must dedicate financial resources to fund the intentional evangelism projects of the local church.

9. POSITIONING THE CHURCH MINISTRIES

In order to understand the process of positioning church ministries for health and growth, it is important to understand God's plan for ministries. In order for ministries to function effectively, they must understand that God's plan for each ministry is to be interdependent and interconnected, not independent and disconnected. The Bible provides many illustrations that reveal how these ministries should work together for a common goal. We have identified two of the most significant illustrations earlier in this book, when we focused on the vision of the valley of dry bones and Paul's comparison of the body of Christ to the human body. In order to be healthy and effective, we must be connected, healthy, and working together!

However, we must also realize that there must be a system for implementing these ministries. **The process of implementing God's plan for ministry should be begin with a simple question: "If the local church congregation should be the representative body of Christ in their community, what ministries should they provide in order to demonstrate a complete and healthy body?"** Another way to ask this question is: "If Jesus was personally standing at the location of our church every week, what type of ministries would Jesus provide or engage in?"

While the actual list of different types of ministries is almost endless, let's briefly identify twelve different types of ministries that each church should have:

Evangelistic, Outreach or Bridge-Building Ministries

These are ministries that are designed to connect the church to the community and the community to the church.

Assimilation Ministries

These ministries are designed to introduce and engage a new person into the life and ministry of the church family.

Discipleship Ministries

These are ministries of the church which are diversified in order to provide an effective process of spiritual formation for every age group (children to senior adults). The goal is to lead believers into various levels of spiritual maturity.

Corporate or Collective Worship Ministries

The worship ministries of the church should be designed to bring together as many different people (different ages, demographics, etc.) for a time of corporate or collective worship, prayer, and receiving the teaching and preaching of the Word of God. Where possible, worship ministries should be multi-generational. Where feasible they should incorporate multiple worship styles, locations, and times.

Small Group Ministries

The small group ministries primarily function to create the opportunity for relationship building within a smaller group of people. However, they may also feature specific Bible study topics or service projects. In order for small group ministries to be holistic, they should include a period of time for building relationships, praying for one another, studying the Bible, sharing life's celebrations and struggles, and introducing unbelievers to a caring small group community where they can come to know Christ.

Specialized Ministries

The specialized ministries of the church should provide the

opportunity to customize various aspects of the mission and purpose of the church (evangelism, discipleship, worship, fellowship, and ministry service) to each age group and language group represented.

Gift-Development Ministries

The gift-development ministries should assist believers in three primary ways:

- Identifying and assessing an individual's ministry gifts, interests, personality strengths, ministry burdens, and passions.
- Providing opportunities for gift development through specific training and equipping classes, mentoring relationships, coaching opportunities, and on-the-job training experiences.
- Offering ministry placement opportunities, allowing the gift development coordinators to review the various experiences and areas of effectiveness to determine the best opportunities for believers to serve with fulfillment and not frustration.

Leadership Development Ministries

The church can never grow beyond its leadership base, therefore a vital key to unlimited growth is to be constantly expanding the leadership base of the church. The church should have specific leadership development ministries for the purpose of identifying and developing new leaders, while also further developing existing leaders.

Prayer Ministries

Prayer ministries should be considered a vital part of the church, allowing those who are specifically called to intercessory prayer to have the opportunity to pray together with others who have a similar passion. While opportunities are provided for all believers to participate in prayer within the corporate prayer ministries of the church, they could also participate in specific times of prayer such as a twenty-four hour prayer vigil.

Stewardship Ministries

While stewardship is a part of the discipleship process, there should also be specific ministries that teach believers the biblical foundations of total life stewardship. The principles of total life stewardship not only incorporate the management of time, talent, and treasure (money), so they can be used for the expansion of God's kingdom, but there must also be the stewardship of relationships, that will allow people to come to know Christ and the local church.

Fellowship and Community Building Ministries

In addition to the small group events and activities which provide the opportunity to build relationships, the church should have specific times which enhance the sense of community and belonging for the entire church. This ministry might include events and activities such as celebrations, festivals, and other church-wide relationship building events. Fellowship ministries may also include pre-service and post-service fellowship opportunities. In some cases, church recreational sports leagues, family fun nights, and special interest or hobby nights may also accomplish the goals and objectives of fellowship.

Facilitating Ministries or the Ministries of Helps

These ministries can be discovered in a variety of ways, and are not limited to, but certainly include:

- Greeters or host and hostess ministries
- Welcome center and information center ministries
- Usher ministry and armor-bearer ministries
- Audio-visual ministries (sound and lighting in all ministry areas)
- Technology ministries (internet, projection systems, computer throughout all ministries)
- Transportation ministries
- Facility maintenance and grounds keeping ministries.
- Emergency response and disaster relief teams

- Office volunteer ministries (mail, phones, copying, money-counting)
- Administrative, accounting, and legal assistance

10. POSITIONING THE CHURCH CALENDAR (SEASONS AND CYCLES)

Every church has seasons and cycles in its ministry, but few churches fully understand the importance of these seasons and cycles, how to anticipate them, and how to maximize each one. In our seminars and assessments, we spend time helping churches understand ministry seasons and cycles. There are two brief applications that I will make in this project.

First, it is important to understand that ministry seasons are a period of time (determined by God) when a ministry typically flourishes, develops, and is at its best. There are seasons of ministry which are more conducive to planting churches, reaching the lost, deepening discipleship, and strengthening relationships within a local church and community. Just as a farmer knows there is an appropriate time to plant, water, and harvest, the church must learn to discern these seasons in their church and community.

Secondly, seasons are periods of time, within which a series of events take place and are completed. A simplified way of distinguishing seasons and cycles is to consider the four seasons of weather (spring, summer, fall, and winter). Although there specific dates on the calendar to identify when these seasons are to take place, we clearly see that leaves don't always start turning color or falling from trees on a specific date; nor does spring's showers or winter's cold automatically begin on a specific day. The general time can be identified, but the actual season varies from year to year.

Separate from each season, multiple cycles are recurring, measured, periods of time; some are shorter ministry cycles, others are longer generational cycles or life cycles. Just as the there are multiple days and nights (cycles) within each calendar season, there are multiple ministry cycles (worship services, classes, activities) within each ministry season. At the same time, life cycles and generational cycles are usually longer periods of time and they may include many ministry seasons.

The life cycle of an organization is described in five basic phases: launch or birth, growth, peak, decline, and death. Each of these phases of the life cycle is common in the experience of churches, organizations, and people. To the degree that a church or ministry can understand the life cycle and detect the phase of its own organization, it may be able to restart the life cycle or embrace the value of a generational cycle.

While most churches and organizations only focus on *life cycles* to understand their health and position themselves for their future, it may be better for them to focus on *generational cycles*. Although most life cycles are illustrated with the final stage of death, here's the actual definition of a life cycle.

"A life cycle is the series of changes in form undergone by an organization (ministry or church) in development (phases), from its earliest stage *to the recurrence of the same stage in the next generation*."

The last stage in a life cycle should not be considered death; it should be the start of another life cycle or generational cycle. At the same time, during the life cycle of a church or organization, there are multiple generational cycles. Churches and ministries should never die; they should continuously birth new churches (generational cycles) and ministries (ministry cycles) that extend the life cycle of the organization. Failure to do so will only permit the natural course of the traditional life cycle to be experienced.

If you borrow the comparison to the human life cycle, then churches should be birthing new ministries and new churches throughout its life cycle, not at the end of its life cycle. Every time a new church begins, or a new worship service, or a new ministry, the church is extending its life cycle and it is increasing the potential for the life cycle of the church to be extended into future generations.

During a person's lifetime, it is not uncommon for an individual to encounter seven generations within their family (i.e., the individual's parents, grandparents and great-grandparents, along with their children, grandchildren and great-grandchildren). Within our life cycle (birth to death), just within our own individual families, we have the potential of encountering six other life cycles (three older before us, three after us). As a person experiences these multiple life cycles, they come to realize there is a link between all seven living generations, as well as the many generations before and the many others after us. Understanding this link will enable a ministry to shift from just living out their life cycle to embracing multiple ministry cycles and generational cycles that will increase and extend the impact and influence of every ministry.

The charting of days, months, seasons, and years, along with an understanding of a church's life cycle, ministry cycles, and generational cycles, will enable a local church to connect the dots on the seasons and cycles of ministry within their church. This will empower the ministry to bear its fruit in its season!

CHAPTER SIX

BEGIN "CONNECTING THE DOTS" IN YOUR MINISTRY

Stop and consider all of the different people in your church and in your community, along with the different resources (equipment and facilities), as well as the different existing and potential ministries of your church. Imagine converting all of those elements into dots and placing them on a single sheet of paper. If you could position each one in its proper place, number them with some sense of priority, and then connect the dots, what image would it create? It would create the vision of your church.

That's what *Positioning Your Church* is all about. It is identifying and assessing all of the "dots" you have to work with within your ministry, developing a Strategic Ministry Action Plan to position all of these resources in an effective process, and connecting the dots (living out your strategic plan), thereby realizing the vision of your church.

> You will never see your vision fulfilled in ministry until you begin to connect the dots.

I recommend that you engage in the *Positioning Your Church* process with a group of key leaders. Recognize that you will never see your vision fulfilled in ministry until you begin to connect the dots. I encourage you to attend a *Positioning Your Church* conference or seminar, host a *Positioning Your Church* conference or seminar for your city, region, or organization, or possibly request a *Positioning Your Church* assessment and coaching service for your church. You can find out about each of these opportunities, as well as other resources that are available at **www.positioningyourchurch.com.**